The Optimistic Autistic: Our Testimony

By Sage

Dedication

This book is dedicated to my husband and our two sons. You are my inspiration, motivation and my dream.

We stand on God's promises.

<u>In Loving Memory</u>

In loving memory of Landous Creek & Virginia (Brogden) Thomas!

Grandma, thank you for supporting and encouraging me to continue writing.

This book is dedicated to your memory.

R.I.P.

Table of Contents

Our Testimony

You cannot have a testimony without going through a test! Over the years, it seems as if I have been thrown every type of test imaginable. The only difference is today I can look back at my past and actually be grateful for it all.

Our struggles, turmoil and life lessons have taught us to be grateful and content with our present. Life is a journey. The challenge is seeing the purpose of your journey and accepting it.

In the beginning acceptance was one of the most difficult tasks to do. It took me almost six years to accept our life's journey.

Parenting is a journey. Being a parent is not a job that we retire from after 18 years. It is more like a life-long commitment. Being a parent to an autistic child presents a set of unique challenges that we were not prepared for.

I began to wonder, "why us?" That is, until God answered, "Why not you?" For some crazy reason, I felt that we didn't deserve the burden that we were forced to bare. My life began to change the minute I realized that nothing in my life was a burden.

Everything was placed in our lives for a purpose. We all have a purpose and a plan. It is up to us to decide if we will follow through and do what is right or if we will give up and hang our head.

It was during the darkest, most painful point in our lives when our purpose was revealed. If you have helped improve the life of one person in your lifetime then you have fulfilled a purpose.

We wanted to do just that, but take it a step further. We are aware that there are many more parents out there who are raising special needs children. It is our hope and prayer that this book will help someone.

It will help you take a look at your own life struggles so that you can see your purpose. Once you have your purpose you will have your strength and determination. We have not and will not give up! And we will not let you give up.

Through the tests, trials and triumphs we were able to build a stronger family foundation. Often times we don't know how strong we really are, until being strong is our only option.

We learned quickly that our tests show where our weaknesses lie. A lack of patience was our greatest weakness and my greatest challenge. There is nothing wrong with having challenges; they can bring about positive results.

This book started as my electronic journal, until I had an epiphany.

When Jordan was initially diagnosed, we felt totally alone and lost. None of our friends had special needs children, so no one really understood what we were going through. We could document our journey and share our experiences with the world.

Maybe someone out there has a special needs child and no one to talk to; no one to say that they understand. Well, although I can't say that I know exactly what you are going through, I can tell you for certainty that you are not alone.

Although it may sound cliché, my goal in life is to enrich the lives of others. What's the point in being here if you are not helping someone?

If our story encourages, motivates or improves the lives of others then we have done our job. I hope that this book encourages you to look at the bigger picture. We are not put on this earth for our own satisfaction.

We are here to do a job. I feel like our job is to testify about God's dedication and the dedication of loving parents. We didn't start this journey encouraged, but seven years into the journey we have more faith and courage than we ever thought possible.

I remember my grandmother telling me that in order to fully experience life you must learn something new each day. She was a wise woman. At the time, I didn't understand what she was saying. Now I understand.

As I look back over the past few years, I can say that although my life has been quite eventful and hectic I have learned and experienced a lot. My children have helped me grow more than anyone or anything.

When our oldest son was born my husband and I were 18 and 19 years old, respectively. We had no idea about parenting or raising children. The moment we looked into those beautiful brown eyes we knew that we had work to do. We knew that it would be a difficult task, but we wanted to show our son that hard work beget a happy life.

I thank him profusely because he was an easy baby. He didn't cry often and he behaved well. He is the most amazing kid. I see my father's calm and easy spirit in him. Aiden was and still is my Angel. In fact, that is what I call him, "Mommy's Angel". Since he is now, 13 years old, I try not to call him that in front of anyone. Sorry son ☺

His temperament and behavior allowed me to multi-task while parenting. I obtained my Associates and then a Bachelor's degree while Aiden was a baby. He encouraged me to do more and that is exactly what I did.

Less than a year after Aiden's birth my nephew Kendrick was born. Our family was growing and everyone was thrilled about the changes. We worked together to raise well rounded children and that is exactly what we have, today.

The "Big Boys" as they are so affectionately called are true gems. They step in and play with their brothers and try to teach them. I couldn't have asked for a better nephew and son.

While they had their challenges, the big boys hit every one of their milestones on or before the desired time. They are bright children with a zest for life. This is why when we found out that we were expecting again, we were overwhelmed with happiness.

Since raising the first one didn't prove to be too trying, we knew that the second child would be even easier. We had already experienced +it. We knew what to do for teething remedies, colic and all the other great things that came with raising an infant.

My sister and I found out that we were both pregnant in late 2004. Her baby was due in May and mine was due in July. We were both looking forward to having new babies in the house and so were our parents.

When my sister was in her third trimester she began to experience breathing issues. When she initially told us about it, we brushed it off as being, "pregnant". As we watched the helicopter air lift my sister from our home hospital to Baltimore, we realized how wrong we were.

My sister spent a month in the hospital. My nephew was born a month early. During this time I remember traveling to work then leaving work and driving directly to Baltimore. Although, I was also in my last trimester of pregnancy I had to be there with my sister.

Adventures of the Babies

A few months later, my sister and her baby came home. All was well. "The Babies", as we affectionately referred to them, were something spectacular. They would do some of the strangest things.

From their first few months on this earth, Kyle and Jordan have been a team. Jordan would do the mischievous work and Kyle would watch, giggling with glee.

At 14 months old, they figured out how to lock the door. My sister walked outside to get the mail. She left the children in the house, only to return to a locked door. My sister sat outside for nearly an hour, waiting on them to let her back inside the house.

My parents constructed a pond in the back yard. The pond was beautiful and filled with fish. Everyone would sit near the pond and relax.

The babies had different ideas. Instead of watching the pond, they decided to jump in for a swim. I'll never forget the frantic call I received from my sister. "Kyle was swimming in the pond!" she exclaimed.

This went on for the majority of the summer until my parents decided to build a fence around the pond. By then, the poor fish were either dead or too frightened to venture to the top of the pond.

Jordan became a 24 hour job for our entire family; you couldn't turn your back on him. Someone had to watch his every move. We soon learned that Jordan watched us for cues. He would wait until we were distracted and make a run for it. This started at the age of three, we are still chasing him.

Before "the Babies" were diagnosed with Autism, we knew that something was different about them. When they were only 2 years old, they called 911. Thinking that an emergency was occurring, naturally they showed up at our home.

My sister called me at work, hysterical. She told me that the police were at the house to check on her well-being. The children called 911 and took the telephone off the hook. Since there was not answer when they tried to call back, they sent a car out to check on her.

While she talked to the police, the babies somehow gained access to the inside of the car. She said they she had to ask the police for help with extracting the boys from the car.

Jordan was famous for tampering with the toilet and clogging it. He would drop his toys in the toilet and flush away. We grew increasingly aggravated about this. Spanking wasn't working, neither was stern talking, nor time out. After replacing the toilet twice and paying countless plumbers, we decided to address the problem differently.

We went the tough love route. Jordan has a special appreciation for action figures. He loves Super Mario Brothers action figures. In fact, every time we visit a store he requests a Mario toy. He keeps them locked safely inside his backpack and carries them everywhere. These were the toys that occasionally found themselves in the toilet.

So, the day I noticed four action figures in the toilet, I instructed Jordan to bring me his backpack. I told him that he was wrong and that I was upset because he did something he knew he shouldn't do. I then made him take every toy out of his backpack and put it in the trashcan in the kitchen.

The look he gave me broke my heart. He looked so hurt. He knew that he was throwing away his prized possessions. It hurt, but the lesson had to be taught.

We were wasting our time and our money. Purchasing toys that ultimately ended up being flushed down the toilet, causing us to spend additional money for repairs. It couldn't go on any longer.

We haven't had a problem with the toilet since then. We are still very cautious of him going in the bathroom alone.

By the time Jordan turned three he could figure out the inner workings of any electronic device. Since his brother was six years older, his influence on Jordan was strong. Jordan watched his brother play video games and soon conquered it.

He loved playing with the Nintendo DS and the Gameboy. If allowed, he would sit for hours and play the handheld game, while Kyle watched happily. I was shocked and amazed the day he saved the princess and won the game. He was so young and yet, showed no emotion as the fireworks exploded and confetti filled the screen.

We were unaware of it at the time, but his love for all things Mario started at three. Although, he wasn't verbal he made his point about Mario. He loved playing the game. We purchased him a Wii the year he turned four. During family gatherings we would turn on the Wii and chuckle as our family stared in amazement.

At the age of four, he was not speaking, but he could win an entire game in less than an hour. We knew that we had a gift in Jordan. My father reminded me constantly that Jordan was a blessed child. He told me that God was going to use Jordan one day. I firmly believe that this is true.

It wasn't long before we realized how truly gifted our son was. My husband had a Washington Nationals hat that Jordan favored. Every time my husband put the hat down, Jordan would quickly grab it and place it on his head. The funny thing was, he would put the hat on backwards. This went on for a while.

Everyone thought we put his hat on like that, but we knew that Jordan was an independent child. We finally took Jordan to the hat store to get his own Washington Nationals hat. After we purchased the hat, the customer service rep placed the hat on Jordan's head. Jordan promptly removed the hat and turned it backwards, as he left the store.

Introducing Jordan

From the moment I felt Jordan kicking in my womb, I knew that he was going to be different. In fact, I remember his first sonogram. I was less than 3 months pregnant, yet Jordan's tiny body was moving constantly on the screen. When I say moving, I mean he was literally flipping his body around. I remember thinking about how odd that was, but I pushed the thought aside.

Jordan came into the world weighing close to 10 pounds. Jordan acted as if he had been here for years before his time.

My aunt came to visit us in the hospital and as she held him on her shoulder, he turned towards her face and looked at her. She exclaimed, "Wow, this boy is looking right at me. How many months is he?" and we all looked at her like she was crazy.

She was quiet for a second and once it registered that he was born not even 5 hours prior to this time, she screamed with laughter.

Jordan and my nephew were christened when they were three months old. At the dinner party after his Christening, he was laying in the floor on a blanket as we sat around in him a circle, just watching him. We watched him lift his head and rock his body from side to side.

Finally after a few minutes of watching him try to roll over on his side, my uncle exclaimed, "I wish he would just roll over." And as we laughed, Jordan rolled over to his side and again to his stomach, kicking his feat as if he was trying to crawl. We all gasped.

At that moment, we all knew that he was different.

Jordan was an exceptional baby. He was sleeping through the night before he turned 2 weeks. He didn't cry a lot and wasn't a fussy baby. He was crawling by four months and by the time he was nine months he had mastered walking.

We noticed that he scowled a lot and he was a very strong baby from the start. We would sit him in the baby swing and watch in awe as he leaned forward in the chair and turned the dial on the side of the swing to make it go faster.

At 5 months he was climbing out of his crib and scaling the side of it.

My husband walked in his nursery one morning, preparing to feed Jordan when he noticed that the crib was completely empty. He looked around the room and noticed Jordan contently playing with his stuffed animals on the floor.

At first, he didn't believe that Jordan had the ability to climb out of his own crib at such a young age, so we put it to the test.

Early the next morning we crept into the doorway of the nursery, planning to witness this extraordinary task and watched Jordan peacefully resting in his crib. We stood there for a few minutes, not wanting to walk away and miss something.

We noticed Jordan sit up in his crib and pull himself into a standing position, using the crib as leverage. Once he was in the standing position, we witnessed him hoist himself over the railing of the crib and scale down. It was amazing.

We didn't know what else to do, so we put in his baby book and told our family. By this time, they thought Jordan was a phenomenon.

When we visited relatives, Jordan would astound them. He would be crawling around the house, pulling himself up on things. He learned how to crawl up and down the stairs so quickly, we had to install a lock on the basement door.

By the time Jordan began walking we had to wear running shoes to keep up with him. He would take off running and you would have to catch him, before he did something dangerous. It was very serious to my husband and me, but to Jordan it was all a game.

We had to install locks on the outside of the bathroom and bedroom doors to keep him out. He enjoyed hearing us complain about the mess he made. We had to baby-proof our entire home.

It also became evident that Jordan had trouble communicating. He would not babble or use baby talk. When he wanted things he would crawl to it or cry for it pointing.

I also noticed around this time that my son was not using vocabulary like other children. Although he made a lot of noise, he would not try to form words.

Kyle was born a month premature so the Infants and Toddlers program would come to my sister's house and visit her and Kyle. One day my sister called me at work to inform me of her recent appointment.

She said that the nurse told her that Kyle had a developmental delay, based on a few assessments that she had conducted on him. At that moment, I thought to myself about my own concerns about Jordan's lack of communication. I told my sister how I was feeling and she offered me the phone number of the program so I could see about Jordan being tested.

I contacted the Infants and Toddlers Department and spoke to someone about Jordan's lack of vocabulary. After a series of questions, the light bulb clicked and I realized the severity of the situation and the possibility that something could be wrong with my son. It hit me like a ton of bricks.

I scheduled an appointment to meet with a representative who would evaluate Jordan to determine if he needed additional assistance.

I met with the representative at my sister's house a few days after I contacted the organization and she proceeded to evaluate Jordan. She conducted a series of assessments to determine his communication and motor skills.

The representative read me the results of her findings at my sister's dining room table. She said that Jordan was developmentally delayed in speech and communication. She said every other assessment of his abilities showed strengths, where communication was the weakest.

I knew that Jordan was different, but I could ignore it up until that very moment. After she read me the results, she asked me if I had any questions for her.

I sat there unable to respond for a few minutes. I looked at my son, watching him as he played in the floor with his toys, wondering what all of this would mean for him and his future.

After they concluded the initial assessment, we visited the Infants and Toddlers Department regularly. We were determined to find a way to help Jordan communicate. Meanwhile, Jordan busied himself with the Nintendo DS and the Wii. We noticed how exceptionally skilled he had become with the video games. He was able to save the princess and beat the majority of the games that he played.

He also played with an intensity that I had never seen in a child. Strangers would remark on how well he played with his games as they stared at him in fascination. It was funny watching this two year old boy with a bottle hanging out of his mouth, playing games on his Nintendo DS like a teenager.

Jordan started in the Intensive Structured Learning Environment (ISLE) Program with his cousin Kyle. Their teacher was phenomenal. In fact, she quickly became a part of our family. She would visit our home regularly to check on Jordan and Kyle. I was very impressed by her ability to keep calm and maintain structure within the household and the classroom.

At the time, Jordan was not the easiest child to teach but she was able to teach him and keep him happy. Jordan was three years old when he started at Beach Elementary School. He attended this school for a year and became comfortable with the program.

Tips from a Formerly Stressed Mom

I learned a lot about Jordan, just by watching him. Without saying a word, we had an understanding. Every time I learned something new I wrote it in a notepad. By the time Jordan turned seven, I had amassed quite a list. In hopes that this may help you with your child, I have detailed some of the lessons that I have learned.

Below are some important ideas to try:

Doctor Appointments

When scheduling doctor appointments make sure to inform the receptionist of any foreseeable issues (e.g. need to be in a quiet area, morning or afternoon preferences, anything that will make it easier on your child during their visit).

Jordan had a problem with sitting still for long periods of time. He hated being in small spaces with a lot of people. He also didn't like walking into a room that was filled with people. I knew that Jordan didn't like doctor offices, but we felt that it was necessary for his growth.

We visited many specialists and doctors during this time, so it didn't take long to realize that something had to be done. Since Jordan didn't react well to doctor appointments, I tried to find ways to accommodate him.

Jordan's doctor overbooked on a regular basis, we often would be stuck in his office for hours. It was horrific, but this was Jordan's favorite doctor. He was comfortable with him. So after a few visits filled with tantrums and disruptions we decided to try a different approach.

We established a system in which they could call me on my cell phone when a room was available for us. We didn't sit in the waiting room at all. This works well for any appointment.

A good day can go sour if your child is unhappy. Why put them in situations in which you know they will not do well?

Shopping

Our visits to the grocery stores were probably the most embarrassing and entertaining. When I took him to the grocery store, he would sit in the cart with his arms outstretched wide enough to knock down the food on the shelves.

He would then, smile with delight as the jars of mayonnaise and the glass jars of pickles crashed to the floor, creating a mess. After a few trips wrought with anxiety and frustration, we finally decided that we had to figure out a better way.

We decided to set ground rules for the stores. Before we left home, we would explain the itinerary for the day to Jordan. I would then, allow him to pick a favorite toy or gadget to carry to the store. I told him that he was responsible for keeping the toy/object safe.

Jordan loved responsibility and thrived when he was given a task. Since we assigned him with the task of choosing a special toy and keeping it safe, he took his job very seriously.

I would place him in the shopping cart and hand him my cellphone, his Nintendo DS or a bag of goldfish.

Whatever he chose before we left the house would accompany him. I spoke to Jordan like he could understand me, because there was no doubt in my mind that he could. I knew that he could understand what I was saying. Just because he wouldn't respond, didn't mean he didn't comprehend.

This was another lesson for me to learn. Never underestimate your child. They are much smarter than many give them credit.

He took his job seriously and paid more attention to the toys in his hand than to the objects on the shelves. We also ensured that he stayed in the confines of the cart at all times. I kid you not, Jordan has not walked in the grocery store since he was a baby.

Now at seven years old, Jordan walks in the store without any assistance. We don't hold his hands now. He needs to feel independent. He craves independence now.

The Schedule

I am a true Scorpio in the fact that I am a self-described, spur of the moment type of person. We loved taking family vacations to the beach, snow tubing and road trips.

For a while we rode an emotional rollercoaster on trips with Jordan. We started our trip excited, but by the end of the vacation we were miserable.

Jordan has truly changed this aspect in me. I lived the first twenty-five years of my life being a spur of the moment person. We soon realized that this type of time management didn't agree with Jordan.

He objected to abrupt schedule changes by displaying negative behaviors (e.g., tantrums, being uncooperative, crying).

At first we thought it would be best if we stopped taking family trips until he was a little older. Then we realized that we were only punishing ourselves.

We decided to take Jordan on family trips and outings again, but with a well-organized plan. We needed to teach him how to behave on trips as opposed to stopping the trips all together.

What was our solution? Plan, Plan, Plan!

Your vacations will go much smoother if you take the time to fully plan each day. A schedule keeps you and your child on track. We keep a dry erase calendar on the refrigerator to keep track of the kids' appointments, vacations and important dates.

I know what you are thinking, "Who has time for that?" But if you fail to plan then you plan to fail. With an autistic/special needs child you don't have the luxury of not planning.

We learned pretty quickly Jordan had a heightened perception of feelings. I realized that if I was in a state of mania for whatever reason, it would also set him off.

This usually resulted in us having a bad day. Through Jordan, I learned to plan my days fully to ensure that I was never in a rush or a hurry.

We learned quite early that informing Jordan of his daily plans helped curb his behavior problems. Although my plans were never rigid, they gave him an estimation of what to expect. Autistic children are driven by their schedule. Jordan seemed to enjoy it and I was less stressed.

It was funny watching Jordan check his schedule in the morning and throughout the day. I felt like his secretary, trying to keep him briefed of his schedule.

Before we left our home we had snacks already prepared and a plan for Jordan. We used a picture system to create a daily calendar for Jordan. As we moved through the day, Jordan moved his picture from each activity. Once he was able to visualize the next step he was more at ease with transitioning.

Jordan's Data Book

When Jordan was initially diagnosed, we immersed ourselves in all things Autism. We exhausted resources and ourselves trying find a way to help him. We visited countless specialists, doctors and researchers.

Each time we visited a doctor we left their office with massive amounts of paperwork. It became quite overwhelming.

We decided to purchase a large 3 ring binder to maintain his paperwork. We filed Jordan's daily communication logs for school, his IEP information and any other helpful information.

I typed a quick blurb about Jordan. I included his likes, dislikes and interests. We also documented a chart with his favorite foods and preferred activities. I organized the notebook using divider tabs and tiny post-it notes.

We started maintaining his notebook when he was three years old. All relevant information remained. Outdated information such as old IEP's and old communication logs were filed away for future reference.

I kept a chart inside the notebook that detailed Jordan's medications, dates prescribed and dosage. We also documented his moods/behavior and eating habits. This way we could tell if something new in his diet or daily life was wreaking havoc.

Since we met with so many different specialists and doctors, this really came in handy for us. This was a major accomplishment because we had all of Jordan's information at our fingertips.

We carried the notebook on every new appointment. The doctors teased us about being overly organized, but they had no idea. This notebook helped streamline our lives.

I scanned the contents of his notebook, so I could keep a soft copy of his medical information. Instead of spending the majority of an appointment getting to know Jordan, we would fax or email his information to the office prior to our visit.

This way the doctor had the opportunity to know Jordan before meeting him.

This idea worked out quite well. We never encountered a physician or specialist who took issue with the notebook. In fact, they were grateful that we were able to provide an overview of Jordan in advance.

Be your own advocate

Advocates are useful to those who do not understand Special Education law and procedures. While some parents are well versed in Special Education law and can move through the process with ease, many are not so lucky. Special Education is quite complicated. Many times an advocate will save you heartache and headache.

There are many people out there willing to help parents and special needs students, however locating these people may be a trying task. As a parent who struggled with locating support from outside of our home, I would suggest that you start at home.

The more knowledge that you can gain regarding your child's disability and their needs, the better armed you will be. Be armed with knowledge.

Know what makes your child tick; know what frustrates your child and what makes them happy. This will not only help your child, it will also help you.

As parents, we must remember that when it comes to our children, we are the first and only advocate. We have a vested interest in our children, where others do not.

The doctor, who services your child, may care about your child, but ultimately they are a physician because of the pay. The pharmaceutical company may provide the vaccines, but they are more driven by money than saving lives.

School Issues

My husband and I grew up in a small town. We loved the simple life that we lived as children so we decided to raise our family in the same town. To us this decision made perfect sense.

Our children could attend the local school system, which had plenty of Blue Ribbon schools. The neighborhoods are still small and family friendly.

Aiden soared in the public school system. He had great teachers that cared about his education. The format fit him and he was able to learn quickly. Jordan on the other hand didn't fare as well in this school setting.

Jordan started school at three years old. His teacher was amazing. Kristal had a way of encouraging the children to play and communicate with each other. He spent his first year with Kristal at the Infant and Toddler Program. Then he moved on to an Integrated Learning classroom and continued to grow.

He had his good days and he had his bad days. Jordan is a very active child so he had a lot of trouble keeping still. He is also a very determined child. I call him my problem solver. If he has something on his mind he will stop at nothing to accomplish it. This is a fantastic trait to have as an adult, however as a child, not so much.

The teachers struggled to make him conform to what they wanted him to do. This usually worked well for them, with any other student. This didn't go over well with Jordan. He rebelled, big time.

He had meltdowns, tantrums and issues that required us to pick him up from school, daily. It was maddening. Everyday someone had to leave their job to pick Jordan up from school.

This went on for weeks, before the school decided to meet about this issue. Their response, "our techniques aren't working, he needs to be in an institution". This was the saddest time in our lives, but it also made our family stronger and ultimately put Jordan in a better spot than he would have ever been.

We are grateful for the things that we had endured to get to this point. We were not so grateful that these things were at Jordan's expense. This is why it is essential for you as the parent to be your child's advocate.

No one else loves your child like you. Understand that no one will invest the time, energy and money in your child like you.

Jordan' s Elementary School Experience

Meanwhile Jordan had been displaying aggressive behaviors in school more frequently. His daily behavior sheets showed that he was angry or sad during the majority of the day. My husband was tasked with the job of picking Jordan up from school every time the teacher or nurse called.

The school system had been experiencing issues trying to hire educated and qualified staff to assist with their special needs students since Jordan was two. We noticed that behavior specialists and special education teacher positions were in a constant state of turnover.

We were introduced to a new behavior specialist towards the end of Jordan's kindergarten school year.

She appeared ambitious and enthusiastic. We were excited and enthused about the upcoming school year. Jordan was recommended for the Extended School Year (ESY) program. This program ensures that a student receives instruction throughout the summer so there is no danger of a student regressing when they were not in school.

We noticed, however that after Jordan started ESY he was constantly being sent home because he removed his patch at school or because he threw a temper tantrum. There were even times that he would be sent home due to incontinence. We couldn't believe it. Jordan has been potty trained for years, he knew better than that. We were quite upset with Jordan.

During an IEP meeting we were informed that Jordan's behaviors were preventing him from learning and progressing in school. We were also informed that the following day would be Jordan's last day in school for a while. The team felt that Jordan should be sent to an inpatient facility for diagnostic purposes. My husband and I were horrified. We sat in the meeting stunned by the details and the accounts that were given about Jordan's daily behaviors.

We were informed that Jordan would need to be home schooled while we awaited a decision from the Kennedy Krieger Institute's Neurobehavioral center. When we left the meeting we drove directly to the gym. We felt that we would have a better chance at dissecting and discussing the entire situation with clear minds. After an hour work out we rode home in silence.

We allowed ourselves the entire day to mourn, whine and cry about our situation. Then the next day, we sprang into action. I contacted Jordan's former teacher from the Infant and Toddler program.

She worked so well with Jordan in the past, and I knew that she would be able to help us. I can honestly say that she was the most instrumental person in motivating Jordan to do his work and to speak. She agreed to meet with us to discuss Jordan.

Over a glass of wine, we informed Kristen of our situation. We informed her that the school personnel felt that our son belonged in the in-patient facility at Kennedy Krieger Neurobehavioral Center. I will never forget the conversation that ensued after this. She informed us that she was currently working with the high school students in the ISLE program.

In this position, she teaches the children how to become independent. She has a classroom of five boys. She takes them to the store with shopping lists and lets them walk the store to purchase the items on their list. She instructs them on how to use their cell phones to improve their communication skills by texting their parents and teachers.

We waited two full weeks before we heard anything from the school regarding our son's home schooling assignment. By the second week, I was so angry and frustrated; I decided that it was time to send an email.

You see, what we didn't know was Maryland State Law a child cannot be removed from school for longer that ten days.

Although, I wanted to lie in my bed and throw the covers over my head, I knew that I could not. We had to do something for our son. I sent an email to the meeting attendees. I informed them that we needed to hear from someone regarding home schooling and we needed to hear from them quickly.

She told us of the opposition that she faced in the school system. The school system is quite antiquated and they rely on the knowledge of individuals who graduated from college twenty years ago. These individuals don't understand that there are new methods out there that they could utilize to reach these children.

She informed us that one of her students had been through the exact same thing. The parents were told to send their child to the Kennedy Krieger Institute and they basically sent him to school each day and he continued to regress. This was not documented as a knock against the institute, more a knock against the parents for allowing the ball to be dropped on their child.

We decided that based upon the conversation with Kristen that we would aggressively pursue alternative options. We knew that our son required assistance with his behavior problems, but we didn't want his behavior to deter his education and academics. We decided that we would have Kristen home school Jordan while we waited on a decision from the Kennedy Krieger Institute regarding behavioral management.

After we sent the email to the Special Education Department we began working towards locating a solution that would fit for Jordan. We decided that he would receive speech therapy and occupational therapy through outside services in conjunction with home school.

We also decided that we would teach Jordan while he remained home. My husband purchased kindergarten instructional tools and began working with Jordan. We set up a visual schedule for Jordan to keep him informed of his daily home school tasks. He seems to be thriving in the home school environment.

He met the majority of his IEP goals at home with Kristen compared to the fact that at school they were unable to address any of the goals.

All autistic children do not learn the same nor do they behave the same. The school was trying to make Jordan fit into the compartment that they established. Jordan is a determined child. He knows the direction that he likes things to go and he will not deviate from his plans.

He is highly intelligent and very teachable, but when the teacher and the student are at odds the environment becomes totally unproductive. This is exactly what occurred in Jordan's class.

We decided that instead of returning Jordan to the school, that it would be best to move him to a program that would better suit his needs. I contacted principals in the school system that I was employed in and attempted to locate a school suitable for Jordan. During this process, I went through a range of emotions.

I was disappointed in myself for not removing him from the school earlier. I knew that he was not progressing as well as he should have and I just thought that it would come.

I kick myself for not being as proactive as I could have been. Then I remind myself that I am only human and that we are doing the best for our sons. We are fighting for our children.

While preparing for Jordan's transition to another school system, he remained on home schooling for 3 months. I felt that this time was perfect for Jordan because he had the opportunity to reprogram himself concerning school.

I didn't want him to hate school. School was a large part of his life and education was something that we prided ourselves on in our family. I want to ensure that our sons had the resources and the opportunities to attend college so that they could have a successful life.

Who says that just because Jordan is having difficulties now in school that in 5 or 10 years he would not improve? The future is totally unknown to us all.

We like to plan for the future as if we control it, but really we can only control ourselves and our reactions to the way things are, we cannot control everything in our lives.

I remember my grandmother telling me constantly that God laughs when we make plans, because he is in full control. I like to believe that. That thought gave me serenity and encouragement.

God has been so good to us, we had no other choice than to have faith in the fact that he wouldn't fail us.

Picture Exchange Communication (PECS)

Jordan's teacher introduced my family to the Picture Exchange Communication (PECS) system. PECS was developed in 1985 by Dr. Andy Body and Speech and Language Pathologist, Lori Frost. It was developed for children and adults who were living with communication and speech impairments.

PECS was developed originally for a program assisting autistic individuals in Delaware, and has now been nationally recognized as an ingenious communication tool.

PECs is a communication system consisting of four phases. The first phase of the system is to teach the student how to exchange the single pictures with a communication partner (usually the teacher or speech and language pathologist).

The second phase involves expanding the PECs system from school to home including relatives, his peers and different places. This teaches the student to be a better communicator outside of the classroom. The third phase involves picture discrimination.

The student is provided with a few picture cards (not all) and are asked to select the picture that displays their favorite things. In Jordan's case, we placed the pictures in his communication book.

The fourth phase involved structuring a sentence. For Jordan, we took pictures of all of the things he enjoyed doing.

We took pictures of his Nintendo Wii, Nintendo DS, his favorite foods, and his favorite outside activities to start the process. During this phase the student learns that they must hand the picture to the teacher when they want a desired item or to do something that they like.

We created a PEC card that was essentially a picture of Jordan and the words "I Want" under the picture. He had to create a sentence, using the other PEC cards, based off of what he wanted to do or eat. We also took pictures of the places that he wanted to go.

We would say it for him and then instruct him to repeat our sentence, based off the card he chose. (e.g. I want goldfish)

The communication book is a small three ring binder or a poster board in our case. The book is lined with strips of Velcro like the actual PECs pictures and the pictures are displayed on the poster board.

We created two boards for Jordan. The first board was his daily schedule, in which the pictures were displayed in sequential order, starting from the time he awoke and progressing through bedtime.

The second communication board displayed his favorite activities, games and foods. This board was referred to as his reward board.

When he did a good job on an activity or had a good day, he would be instructed to choose a reward picture from the board, hand the picture to us and we would give him his requested reward.

This system allowed Jordan to communicate his wants, needs and dislikes to his teachers and his family using a series of pictures. In fact, we created a daily schedule for Jordan using the PECS system.

The schedule consisted of pictures that displayed each activity that he would be expected to do during the day.

For instance, his home schedule started with a picture of him in bed sleeping, then we showed a picture of him waking up, the next picture was of Jordan brushing his teeth and washing his face.

Each step that we wanted him to take was depicted in brightly colored images. Each picture had a Velcro backing that attached to the daily schedule board. This made it easy to make adjustments to his schedule if something abruptly changed.

Jordan became quite comfortable with this method.

Although, his way of communicating with us was out of the ordinary, we loved the idea that he would be able to communicate. We came to understand that Jordan was going to be completely extraordinary and in order to raise an extraordinary child, you must take extraordinary measures.

Although, the process was not always smooth and it involved a vast amount of patience and determination, we were able to get Jordan to utilize the system effectively. In the beginning of the process I remember Jordan having more tantrums than usual. I soon realized that his tantrums were also a form of communication.

He wanted us to know that he did not want to use the cards to communicate. He enjoyed the fact that I could tell based on his whine, points or gestures, exactly what he wanted. He didn't have to put in very much effort when I was doing everything for him, based off of mother's instinct.

But in order for me to teach Jordan the system, I had to go through the heart-wrenching process of ignoring his cues and reinforcing the PECs system.

He had a habit of walking up to me grabbing my hand and placing it on whatever he wanted, or pointing to what he wanted and standing patiently as I obliged.

Jordan taught us that in order to help him, you must first understand him and his situation. He was unable to communicate in the way that we were used to communicating, verbally. So, to communicate with Jordan you had to utilize alternative methods. Once he understood the methods, the sky was the limit for Jordan.

I recall, observing him during his school work session, one day. I was so impressed by the way he utilized the PECs system to communicate with his teacher and the speech and language professionals.

He showed me his schedule by pointing at each picture while saying what each picture represented. I sat at the small table in the tiny chair, beaming with pride. Jordan gave me a reason to work hard at something.

At that moment I knew that I would give my all to ensure that my son had the education that he deserved and required. I knew that while others felt like my son would not progress, I knew that he would do far greater than anyone would every conceive.

He had to do better or I would essentially have failed as his mother and protector.

Help them understand

Not knowing is ignorance, knowing and not caring is stupidity.
By the time Jordan turned three he was close to 40 pounds and had the strength of a teenager. He was a strong and independent child.

Although, he was still very limited in communication, Jordan made sure that he got his point across. His tantrums were becoming more frequent. During this time, I was completing my final year in graduate school and had recently been promoted to a new position.

Our house was in a constant sense of chaos and duress. Jordan had energy like no other. He would awake at 6:00 a.m. each day and although his bedtime was scheduled for 8:30, he would not fall asleep until after midnight. My husband and I were concerned about his lack of sleep.

We couldn't let him out of our sight. We had to do everything in shifts. There had to be an adult with eyes on Jordan at all times. I refer to him as, "Tas". He is my Tasmanian devil. The moment his feet hit the floor he was going at 70 mph. In his wake lay broken dishes, toys, destroyed furniture and my tears.

We purchased a new living room set when he was born. By the time he was three the set was completely damaged and in need of replacing. Jordan had a habit of jumping on the couch.

One day I noticed that the springs in the couch were totally destroyed. I couldn't believe it. I watched my three year old remove the seat cushions from the coach and gleefully jump directly on the springs.

This was one of those times in my life where I felt bi-polar. It was maddening. I would be angry with him for doing something so mischievous, but amazed at the fact that he could figure out something like that.

He knew that he would jump higher directly on the springs. I couldn't help but wonder about the inner workings of Jordan's active mind.

Inquisitive from the start, he was constantly trying to do something out of the ordinary. It frustrated us because generally it was something destructive. I would receive calls throughout the day, informing me that he flushed something down the toilet, stopping it up or he threw something at the window and caused it to break.

I remember the day I received a frantic call from my sister, that they had to contact the fire department because he put his toy in the gas fire place and no one noticed it.

They put my son and nephew down for their nap and soon smelled the smoke. My mother's basement was covered in soot. Oh that was a horrible time.

If it wasn't for our families, I have no idea how we would have survived. They all pitched in to help. Although, we were hesitant at first, family was offering to babysit for us. My mother in law, sister and aunts babysat for us so that we were able to get away.

Although, family offered to keep Jordan we knew that they had their hands full. So, instead of allowing them to help us, we turned them down. Talk about burn out. My husband worked weekends, leaving me home with the children during the day.

For a while we felt guilty about leaving Jordan. We would talk about the children the entire time that we were away from them. Then we realized that if we didn't get a break we would fall apart. We needed to be refreshed. My husband joined the gym as a form of respite. I turned to my first love, writing.

How did we make it through this difficult time? We stopped seeing our situation as difficult and started seeing it for what it was…..LIFE! There was nothing that you could do to change it. We had to change our reactions to LIFE situations.

I can equate my son's condition to someone entering a foreign country. How would you feel if you had to live in Spain and never studied Spanish?

How would you react when you had a question or a need and could not verbalize it? This is how I assume my son feels. He has so much to say, but he cannot translate it so that we can understand it.

Our son is the first autistic person that people who we know have come in contact with. They don't know what to expect. They don't know what to say. We have arrived at events only for Jordan to have a meltdown and have to leave fifteen minutes later.

I can't tell you how often we were asked about Jordan's behavior. We decided that the best way to answer their questions about Jordan was to gather information regarding Jordan's condition and explain it to them.

We wanted to ensure that everyone we came in contact with understood ADHD and Speech delays. I wanted to make sure that they didn't blame the parent or the child for something that neither of us could control.

Do you have any control over cancer, preventing a heart attack, or asthma? No, you cannot control those illnesses, just like you cannot control ADHD or developmental delays. It just happens.

In life, you have to deal with what is given to you. I like to think that this is a test in our lives; to see how we handle a child that the world tells us is imperfect.

My best friend gave birth to her first child and I desperately wanted to see her and the new baby. I decided that after work one day, I would take my sons to visit her in the hospital. When we arrived at the hospital, Jordan was very agitated.

I didn't understand his agitation at the moment but as I look back on it, I know for sure that he was overwhelmed. I had to literally pull Jordan into the hospital room to visit her and the new addition to our family. When we walked into the room I noticed that it was quite crowded with her family.

There were over 15 people there talking and chatting. For anyone else, walking into this type of a situation would not cause them any anxiety, but an autistic person is a different story.

My son immediately became agitated. He started running around the hospital room in circles. I looked around and noticed how her family was staring at him. In fact, she had a sour look on her face as well. She stared at my son shaking her head as if it was such a shame that he was acting in such a bad way.

I am not a mind reader, but based on the looks on their faces I could tell exactly what they were thinking. "She can't control her bad child."

Finally my best friend's sister turns to me and asks if I had him tested for ADHD. Aiden was diagnosed with ADHD and he was very hyper, but he didn't have the tantrums and behavior issues that Jordan exhibited.

Before I could respond to her question, she and the people in the room began to laugh. I realized that the question was not really a question, but a joke.

I took Jordan's hand and said good-bye to my friend, never having the chance to hold the baby. As we quietly walked to the car, my head was spinning. I couldn't believe that my best friend and her sister would treat my son and me the way they did. I sat in my car terribly disappointed by the entire incident, but I didn't want to show the disappointment on my face and upset my boys.

I plastered a happy smile on my face and happily announced that we were heading home. No one knew that I sat in the bathroom late that evening and cried. I felt like my family was robbed.

My husband and I were robbed of a normal and comfortable life. Aiden was robbed of being a big brother to an "ideal" younger brother. I felt horrible. I felt like my life had been cursed. Why me? Why us?

I allowed myself to wallow in self-pity for an evening. As I said my prayers that evening before bed, I promised myself that the next day would be better. I woke up the next day with a sense of renewal and determination. I started to develop a plan for Jordan. We knew that Jordan required assistance with his behavior issues and with communication.

So the next day, I researched ways to help my son. I located a wonderful doctor who practiced at Johns Hopkins Hospital and at our local hospital. I figured that this was as good a time as any to get answers for our son's condition. I called and scheduled his appointment. I didn't let it deter me, when the receptionist informed me that there was a three month wait to visit this doctor.

I used this time to fully educate myself in ADHD and developmental delays. I also became stronger with my responses to people when they talked about my son. No matter what he did or how he acted he still was mine and I had to protect and defend what was mine. I called my girlfriend and informed her that I was hurt by the way her family acted towards my son. She didn't understand and I didn't expect her too.

So instead of becoming angry with her, I emailed her a few of the articles that I had been reading about ADHD and special needs children with behavior problems. I wrote in the body of the email how I truly felt. I told her that I loved her and her family. We had been friends since the sixth grade. I informed her of the trouble that we were experiencing concerning his behavior and his speech delays. I bombarded her with information.

She responded, thanking me for the information and apologizing for her family's behavior. She asked questions about Jordan and I could tell that my email had really hit home with her. That was my goal. I didn't want her to feel awful.

I also didn't want to be angry or hurt any longer. During this time, what I needed more was a friend, someone to confide my feelings in. So I needed her to be on my side instead of my opponent.

You can't judge people based on what they don't know. You must inform them and teach them; make them feel as if they are a part your struggle and your journey.

You will be surprised at how many people reach out to you. You may also be surprised at who you can help through your story.

Beyond the Diagnosis

The months flew by and we grew increasingly anxious and concerned. We had to find out why our son was behaving this way. Our friends had children around the same age as Jordan and they didn't behave in this manner at all.

Jordan did not appear to have progressed verbally. He was able to do everything else, besides talk. My husband took Jordan to the doctor's office and the doctor evaluated him for two full hours.

A month later, his office contacted me and informed me that he was ready to discuss the results with me. I met with the doctor on a rainy October day. By then Jordan was a few months away from his birthday.

I sat down in the office and the doctor told me in no uncertain terms that my son had Autism. He said that Jordan was on the Autism Spectrum. I looked at him like he had grown two heads when he told me the results.

I knew that my baby had a speech delay and I assumed that he was ADHD because he was quite active and aggressive, but Autism....never. Aside from the story that I read about Autism, I had never heard much about it.

The doctor showed me a scale that he documented regarding the Autism spectrum. When I thought about Autism I recalled a story about a doctor and a pianist who had been diagnosed with the condition, and they became successful. I tried not to let myself become discouraged. I asked the doctor if my son would ever talk.

He shook his head indicating that it was doubtful that he would speak or do anything that a "normal" child could do. I listened to him as tears slowly fell down my cheek. This was not the future that I intended for my son. I told him about the story that I had read about the successful autistic people. He dismissed my comments like they would not happen for my son. I left his office feeling overwhelming sadness.

When I left the doctor's office, I had to document a 20 page research paper on Emerging Technologies for my graduate school course. For the first time in my life, I actually wanted to give up. I wanted to throw in the towel, throw my hands up and just give up. During this time, I lost between 30-40 pounds.

I gave this situation too much of me. I know that sounds strange, coming from a mother. Your children are supposed to be all of you, right? I bet the person who lives by that adage is currently miserable and I bet their children can tell.

I stopped concerning myself about food and the necessities. My life became non-existent aside from work and Jordan. I felt lost, alone and hopeless. I didn't know what else to do. I can honestly say that this was the lowest time in my life.

I spent many weeks, wallowing in my own self-pity. Jordan's teacher suggested that we visit the Kennedy Krieger Institute to see if we could find help for Jordan.

I researched the facility and found out that they had an entire hospital dedicated to Autism, the Center for Autism and Related Disorders (CARD).

It took an additional three months for our initial appointment. We took leave from our jobs and made the two hour journey from home to Baltimore.

Jordan was evaluated by the Behavioral specialist in the center. They requested that we bring his other documentation with us concerning his other diagnosis and the services that he was currently receiving. It took them no time to read the previous doctor's evaluation and second it.

The good thing about this center was, they provided resources and testing services. They had a school where students could receive Applied Behavioral Therapy Services to assist with behavior and communication. The downside was that they were located a full two hours away from us.

Although the driving distance was a deterrent, I enjoyed the fact that this new doctor actually explained Autism in depth to my husband and me. She took the time to provide us with brochures and additional information concerning Autism.

The Kennedy Krieger Institute also provides patients with social workers, to help smooth over the process of acquiring additional services and resources.

The doctor explained that patients are diagnosed with autism when they display symptoms across the three major areas of communication, social interaction and repetitive patterns of behavior or interest.

As I listened to the explanation, I could immediately identify with Jordan's love and obsession with Mario and Super Mario Brothers.

Many of those on the Autism spectrum experience difficulties with social interaction as well as understanding social implications and conventions.

I also learned that there is a significant difference between those diagnosed with Autism and those diagnosed with Aspergers.

Asperger syndrome is on the Autism spectrum; however individuals display completely different behaviors than Autism. Individuals with Aspergers meet their language milestones timely, but they also have social interaction difficulties.

Most individuals with Aspergers Syndrome are also highly intellectual or display exemplary talents.

Pervasive Developmental Disorder (PDD) is also a disease on the Autism spectrum. This condition is also identified once a child turns 3. Parents tend to notice at this age, that their child is not progressing normally.

Children with PDD also experience significant developmental delays, in communication, walking and motor skills.

Without generalizing the condition, it has been noted that most children with PDD have strengths in some areas and display developmental delays in other areas.

For example, I noticed that while Jordan was not verbal, he was a sponge when it came to teaching him things. I was typing a research paper on the laptop and he was sitting next to me watching my fingers move across the keyboard.

I noticed that he was intrigued, so I stopped typing and gently took his hand and showed him how to use only his pointer finger and gently glide it across the track pad of the laptop.

Using my right hand, I pointed in the direction of the mouse pointer on the screen as my left hand moved across the pad. Then I asked him if he wanted to try it.

Although, he did not respond, I could tell that he wanted to try it. He let me move his finger around the mouse pad. He laughed with glee as the mouse moved across the computer screen.

After I completed my research, he pointed to the laptop. I asked him, "Would you like to use the laptop?" he smiled at me in response so I repeated, "Laptop" he responded with "Laptop" and took it from my lap.

He immediately started using the laptop with the track pad like a pro. He is such a wiz with the computer, I remember when Aiden was trying to log into the computer and he asked me what the password for the computer was. I told him that he would have to wait until I finished the dishes so that I could log into the computer for him.

When I heard Aiden say, "Thanks Jordan", I went into the living room to see what Jordan had done. Aiden told me that Jordan took the computer from him and clicked on the 'Guest' account so that Aiden could use the computer. I just stood there with my mouth agape, in total shock. He was only 3 years old and he was troubleshooting the computer for his 9 year old brother.

At that point I realized that Jordan could do anything he wanted to do. I decided then that I would never allow Jordan to be placed in a box again. I would not allow others to determine based off of their own checklists and tests. We are better defined by our response to our weaknesses.

As the months progressed, we watched as Jordan became more independent. We realized that Jordan learned by watching us do things and then he tried it for himself. If he wanted popcorn, he didn't wait for us to get it for him.

Jordan has an amazing amount of upper body strength. He would hoist himself on the counter, walk to the top cabinet, where the popcorn was located and open the package of popcorn. Then he would place it in the microwave and hit the button on the microwave labeled "Popcorn".

Jordan was the only four years old child that could win a chin up contest against an adult. He is just that strong. When we go grocery shopping he must carry a bag in the house. This started when he was two years old. Now he carries gallon jugs of water inside without anyone asking and with ease.

He is a very helpful child. Thanks to my sister's tutelage and years of watching her clean a house from top to bottom, Jordan is a great cleaner. He knows how to sweep, wipe tables and use the small handheld vacuum cleaner. He is truly amazing.

We have to remind ourselves and others that just because Jordan has a speech delay it does not mean there is a problem with his cognitive abilities. He has a heightened ability of perception. I tell my friends that Jordan will make an exceptional therapist. He knows what makes us tick and what makes you angry.

He also has no problem using these things against you, when needed. If you do something that makes him angry, you can rest assured that the things you care most about will be damaged, destroyed or thrown in the trash. That's Jordan.

At age two he figured out that I care about my hair products. Imagine my surprise when I awoke one morning to find all of my products scattered across the lawn.

Imagine yourself relaxing on the couch. Then a smell hits you. It's your favorite perfume. Terror erupts in your heart as you race upstairs to find that your child has poured all of your perfume on top of your bed.

Imagine eating the delicious meal that you prepared only to realize that it tastes funny. That's when you notice the empty bottle of dish detergent lying on the floor in the kitchen. Yes, your child has taken the liberty of pouring dish detergent all over the chicken that you just baked for dinner.

When we visited friends, he greeted their children with slaps to the face. Instead of playing with kids at the playground, he would chase them around the playground, playing his own version of tag. Even if the children weren't interested in playing. He just didn't seem to understand the concept of playing nicely. So, we stopped taking him around other kids.

He didn't understand the concept of waiting his turn. I remember the day that we took him to the pool. Since he was only three we took him to the kiddie pool section. The minute he saw the slide he pulled away from me and started running to the slide. I tried to run to catch him but he quickly moved the children out of the way and jumped on the slide. Imagine the evil stares I received from that incident.

I decided the best thing was to stop taking him to the pool until he could behave better.

No one understood. Everyone thought that I was embarrassed of Jordan or I was causing him to behave the way he was behaving. They just didn't understand.

Birthday parties were so much worse. He would chase the kids down. He didn't understand taking turns so he screamed, cried and tantrum while he waited his turn. By the time it was his turn, he didn't want to play any longer.

It was literally exhausting. So we stopped taking him to birthday parties. In short, we became a family of hermits. We used to enjoy parties, cook-outs and family outings. That was all before Tas came on the scene.

I lost a great deal of friends during this time. At the time, I was so consumed with Jordan that I didn't realize their absence. People didn't understand why we couldn't come to their children's birthday parties or why we never invited anyone to our home. It was just too much.

An additional person in our home caused complete and utter chaos for us. Jordan would be over stimulated and act completely irrational. I didn't want to be in my own home, why would I invite others to share in the chaos? No one understood when I tried to explain so, I stopped explaining.

There were the pseudo-experts who felt the need to inform me that there was nothing wrong with Jordan, he behaved that way as a result of me:

- Not talking to him enough
- Not spanking him enough
- Not bringing him around people enough
- Worrying about him too much
- Stressing him out about his behavior
- Focusing on his behavior too much

These were the times where I grew closer to God. I needed an answer as to why things were so difficult in our lives. Why us?

Increased Awareness

After months of stress, pressure and tears we decided to find our own way. We tried to be positive about Jordan and his condition. We tried to anticipate the things that would overstimulate him. We also realized some of the triggers that would prove to upset Jordan. I would assess a situation completely, before I included Jordan in it to ensure that he was comfortable.

Before agreeing to an event, I asked how many people would be there, Jordan didn't like crowded situations. I would ask about the noise level at events.

I found that this type of strategy proved to have 50/50 results because; I would not foresee every event that could set him off.

My uncle informed me that I was trying too hard to anticipate certain things and it would just be best to allow Jordan to be himself.

He became set in his ways at 4 years old. Jordan is a determined child, in the sense that he will not let the opinions or actions of others deter his thinking or his ambition towards doing something. As an adult, this trait is very powerful and can lead to major successes down the road.

But as a child this is one of the most difficult behaviors to deal with. Jordan cannot stay within a normal school setting. We were at the point where we had to really consider having Jordan moved from the public school setting in favor of a more confined private school environment.

One week prior to the first day of school, the behavior specialist and special education director visited my family at home. I am still unsure if the purpose of the visit was to put our fears to rest regarding the start of a new school year or if it was a chance for the behavior specialist to manage our expectations concerning Jordan remaining in the public school environment.

Due to his limited communication skills, Jordan was recommended for Extended School Year (ESY) during the summer. During the meeting, we soon learned that Jordan had not received any instruction, throughout the entire 6 weeks that he was being transported to and from school each day.

"His behavior prevented him from learning", is what we were told. Those words resonated within me.

My husband and I were beyond frustrated with this situation. You feel powerless in these types of situations. Who do you call? There is truly no other person on this earth that knows how you feel when a teacher tells you in plain words that they are not sure if they can educate your child.

I allowed myself one full day to feel sorry for myself and my son. I wallowed in my own self-pity and cried a lot that day. I believe that every person should allow themselves the opportunity to grieve bad news or a bad situation. In my 30 years on this earth, I have realized that I no longer want to be a "Super Woman" I just want to be me. I want to allow myself the opportunity to be an emotional wreck when I need too.

I find that if you allow yourself time to grieve and wallow and give yourself a time limit, your response to the situation will improve. I have done this many times and found that this particular method produces the desired results. Jordan taught me this.

After I wallowed and cried, I had a glass of wine and enjoyed a card game with Aiden and Jordan. We played and joked around like kids and I thoroughly enjoyed placing the school situation involving Jordan, far in the back of my mind.

I have also become cognizant of Jordan's feelings concerning school and activities surrounding it. It has become my goal to make sure that my children receive the best education possible, but I also want them to have a fun filled childhood.

That weekend I took Jordan on a play date with a few of his classmates. I planned for Jordan to run, I dressed comfortably and wore running shoes for that purpose. Jordan also taught me how to plan for an occasion and dress accordingly.

The play date was scheduled on a Saturday, but I spent the majority of the evening Friday in preparation mode. I had our clothes laid out and packed a few of Jordan's favorite snacks.

While Jordan was preparing for his bedtime routine, we discussed his upcoming play date. I made sure that I explained everything step by step. Jordan also taught me that he processes things different.

Some people loved surprises and others do not, Jordan did not enjoy surprises. I showed him a picture of the museum and told him where we would be going and how long we would be there.

We visited the Marine Museum. Jordan had a good time exploring the museum. He was anxious to get away from me so that he could explore on his own.

I was very good about holding his hand and keeping a firm grasp on him at all times. One of the children broke away from the group and took off running towards the picnic area.

As his mother chased him down, I along with the other mothers breathed a collective sigh of relief. Each of us had been through this situation many times before and we were relieved for the moment that we were not chasing after our child, screaming his name as he ignored us and ran faster.

We decided that it would be best to follow the mother in distress to the picnic area. I loved the fact that we had an organized group of women and we were all dealing with the same issues with our children. We didn't have to worry about stares and comments from others when our child took off running or during the time when an unexpected tantrum occurs.

We watched our children run and chase each other around the picnic tables, in pure delight. It was fantastic watching the children laugh and run. Watching Jordan play with his friends I remarked to the other mothers that it was wonderful watching the children be children.

They agreed and we watched them for a few minutes, each of us on our own set of pins and needles, awaiting the next episode.

Sometimes I wonder if our anticipation of the worse is conveyed to the children, because Jordan immediately did what I was secretly praying that he wouldn't do.

He struck one of the children in the face, for no apparent reason. I felt horrible. I apologized profusely to the mother firs; then I took Jordan's hand and asked him to apologize to his friend Joshua.

Jordan would not apologize and he hit Joshua again. At this point I was prepared to take his hand and leave. I made him apologize by prompting each word and telling him to say it to Jordan. I knew that those words were not Jordan's, but I didn't want him to think that striking another person was acceptable.

I took him by the hand and made him sit next to me as he watched the other children run and play, he grew angry and unsettled. Then suddenly, he jumped up from his seat and took off running.

The back of the museum consists of a few piers situated over the Chesapeake Bay. Jordan grabbed a water bottle off the table and ran toward the water's edge. My heart dropped into my shoes, I just knew that he would jump in the water.

I watched in sheer horror as Jordan threw the bottle of water into the Chesapeake, in front of a crowd of people. I didn't know what to do. I could hear the crowd gasp as he tossed the water bottle. I wanted to leave him right there on the pier and disappear.

I could hear my sister in the background screaming to me that she had my purse and keys. I smiled to myself, knowing that she could sense the fact that I was ready to leave.

I was so angry with Jordan and I knew that he could tell.

As I drove my nephew, sister and son to the store, Jordan did not say a word. When we arrived at the store he made sure that he stayed close to me and he reached out for my hands when I wasn't holding his.

My sister remarked that Jordan knew that his behavior had upset me and she could tell by the way he was behaving. I was still very upset with him, but once I looked at his sad eyes, I could tell that he was disappointed in himself.

I knew that Jordan did not want to act that way, but he had aggression built up within him that caused him to react in such a way.

I thought back to the few minutes after he hit Joshua. If I had made him apologize and allowed him to continue to play he would have continued on without incident.

I looked back on the incident, realizing my contribution to his frustration and my own. *Introspection can be a lifesaver.* I had to look at my method of correction and discipline.

My reaction to him hitting Joshua was pure frustration. I was angry and I know he could instantly tell. He in turn responded with the same level of frustration that I displayed. Jordan behaved as if our emotions were one. That had to change.

My refusal to let him play and enjoy himself caused him to become angry and react. I didn't vocalize it though, especially not in front of Jordan. I am not sure if my rationalization of the events were acceptable for Jordan to overhear.

I don't ever want him to think that he is right in striking someone. I want him to understand that there are consequences to everything he does. I decided after that if Jordan reacts in a negative way towards someone then his consequence would be immediate removal, instead of time out.

Jordan teaches me many things on a daily basis. He truly is a challenge and a joy in the same.

DAN Doctors, Psychiatrists, Therapists and Specialists…..Oh My!

Jordan was experiencing many difficulties within the classroom and school environment. The majority of the problems stemmed from behavior and aggression. We tried many different behavior related therapies and behavior modifications.

We tried to get medication from his primary doctor. Our oldest son took medication during his early school years to help keep him focused.

When we initially took Jordan to Kennedy Krieger Institute for help regarding his behavior, the doctor stared at us in shock and amazement. She had never seen a child as unique as Jordan before.

He climbed on top of her bookshelf and leaped to the floor. The doctor's reaction was priceless. We spent over two hours in her office; describing all of the things that Jordan was capable of doing and discussing his limitations.

The tall slender doctor quickly whipped out her notepad and began writing a prescription for our beloved son. My husband and I smiled, happy that someone finally understood our Jordan and they were willing to help.

After the initial visit we were scheduled for monthly visits to check Jordan's progress.

By the fourth month, my husband and I were totally exhausted from the 2 hour drive and the 3 hour doctor visits on top of his weekly speech therapy and occupational therapy appointments.

It was becoming a full time job to help Jordan succeed. We also noticed that none of the treatments or methods that were suggested had proven to be successful for Jordan.

We decided that it would be best for Jordan and our own mental health to discontinue the visits to Baltimore. It saddened us to realize that we had tried something else that did not work for him.

We were so exhausted from researching and identifying new ways to help Jordan, but we knew that we had to continue trying. Jordan deserved our perseverance and persistence.

During this time Jordan was attending the ISLE program at Dares Beach Elementary. While we were aware of Jordan's behavior issues at home, his teachers were scrambling to find ways to assist him in the classroom.

During a marathon type IEP meeting with the teachers and Special Education staff, we decided that Jordan required medication to help him relax and focus so he could absorb that entire he was being taught his lessons in class.

Unfortunately, the medication she prescribed didn't work on him. Instead of calming him he started having weird tics. So we took him off the medicine immediately and moved on.

It was so disheartening, medicating a four year old. We were at our wits end by the third prescription. So, we decided to take another route.

We began researching homeopathic remedies to help Jordan with his hyperactivity and anxiety. Homeopathy or homeopathic medicine is a form of medical practice that heals without the use of prescription medications. Homeopathic doctors use healing qualities from plants, minerals and acids that naturally help the body heal.

We searched for the combination of Autism and homeopathy and found information about Defeat Autism Now (DAN) doctors. The information was so great that we decided to explore it further.

I scheduled an appointment for Jordan with the DAN doctor. We were referred to a wonderful doctor who also had a child on the spectrum. We found her to be quite informative.

She gave us information on how the body can respond to foreign foods that are not organically grown. For example, if someone ate the wrong foods for their body (processed foods or foods with sugars and high fructose corn syrup) the body tries to digest and utilize the nutrients from the food. These ingredients are foreign so the body treats them as such.

The manufactured ingredients are not really nutrients so they have no real place to go. They are considered toxins and invade the bloodstream. Once the toxins are in the bloodstream they begin to travel throughout the body causing all types of issues.

In some cases it could be high blood pressure or cholesterol issues, in children on the spectrum it causes cognitive and behavioral related issues.

DAN doctors generally apply nutrition and behavior therapy to the treatment plan of a child or adult on the spectrum.

They believe that medications are a toxin in their own right, so they often times do not prescribe medications for their patients. Many DAN practitioners prescribe nutritional supplements such as vitamins, amino acids and Omega 3s. They suggest diets that are gluten and dairy free and suggest diets full of organic and farm raised foods.

The main goal is to get the individual back to basics and to sift out the toxins within the body that are affecting the health and behavior of a patient. DAN practitioners also suggest testing to determine if the patient has allergies that may cause problems with their digestive system or their neurological system.

In some cases, the doctor may suggest detoxification therapy, which removes heavy metals utilizing a chelation process. The chelation process is a hazardous procedure, but in many cases parents are desperate to find help for their children and are willing to try anything that may help.

DAN doctors receive a full day of training on DAN related services and treatments prior to receiving their credentialing as a DAN doctor. The doctor that we had the pleasure of meeting was also a pediatrician and saw patients who were not on the spectrum as well as those who were.

It worked out perfectly for my family because the nurses working within the facility had met children like Jordan before and they were not at all surprised by my request at our first appointment.

Upon scheduling the appointment I informed the nurse of my son's condition and requested that they place us in a room to wait for the doctor as opposed to leaving us in the sitting room. This method proved to work well for Jordan.

We prepared Jordan for the appointment two days prior to the appointment, by informing him that he would be visiting a doctor. We found that informing Jordan of any deviances from his usual daily schedule in advance proved to make the new appointment or new event less intimidating and overwhelming for him.

I find that I can now anticipate how Jordan will respond to certain situations. That anticipation alone helps me be proactive in managing his frustration levels before he became frustrated. I have declined many invitations to places that I knew would be too overwhelming for Jordan.

We knew that events held at parks and open areas with more than 20 people are overwhelming for Jordan, so we didn't take him to those events. We have had many people chastise us on the way we "isolate" Jordan.

I have also found that ignoring people and doing what is best for my son and my family prove to be affective. You will learn in your daily life as a parent that people have opinions and suggestions for situations that they really have no clue about.

It is always best to take care of yourself and your family first and foremost. This is the method that I subscribe too.

We attempted this diet with Jordan for a few months and found no real results. Although, many of the parents in Jordan's class and playgroups raved about the DAN diet, we found it to be quite expensive and difficult to convince a child to eat something organic. Children are brand driven from birth.

When Jordan wanted cereal, he asked for Cheerios and he looks for the honey bee on the front of the box. We tried to purchase gluten free Cheerios substitutes. Jordan read the box as if he had been reading for years and handed it back to us without tasting the cereal.

We figured that we could incorporate the other items into his diet secretly. We purchased hundreds of dollars' worth of organic and gluten free products, only to realize that our dear son only ate Cheerios, cheese, ham, eggs, pizza, French fries and chicken nuggets.

He was not planning on deviating from this particular eating plan. So after months of trying and begging on our end, we ended up consuming the organic, gluten free, casein free foods that were meant for Jordan, while he watched us with a humorous smirk on his face.

After three months, we decided that the expensive diet was not suiting our needs or Jordan's, so we decided to scrap that idea and start on something new.

We also tried offering Jordan supplements, hoping that it would assist him with his behavior. We spent hundreds in the Vitamin Shoppe and GNC purchasing pro-biotic supplements, vitamins and minerals, only to find that Jordan would not take them.

It became a game, an expensive game albeit, but a game of sorts where we would try to find ways to hide the vitamins and supplements in Jordan's juice and foods and we would wait to see if he would take them.

We were reminded of how keenly intelligent Jordan really is. He wasn't easily tricked Jordan had become. Jordan would smell his juice and evaluate it before he would take a sip. If he thought something was in it he would move the drink out of his way, indicating to us that he was not planning to drink it.

After a few weeks of this fiasco, Jordan began refusing anything that was not prepackaged. He only drank Capri Suns or juice boxes, because he knew that we would not be able to put anything in those items. We were defeated in that arena so we began researching again.

We were referred to a brilliant genetics doctor. He evaluated Jordan and met with my husband and I to discuss Jordan's condition. To our surprise he informed us that Jordan was not Autistic, but he believed he had a high level of testosterone in his system. He explained that the vaccinations administered to young children contain mercury and other toxins.

The body does not properly filter these toxins, because they are totally foreign and the mercury stores in the cells of the body, affecting everything from brain firing and triggering to hormone levels.

As a result, testosterone being a natural hormone in the body becomes elevated, causing symptoms such as rage, unusual strength and behavior problems. Jordan displayed the same symptoms, we had to give it a try.

Dr. Gyere informed us that all vaccinations contain a form or level of mercury for preservation purposes. He said that he was in a meeting with other practitioners and was questioned about his findings concerning vaccinations and the link to autism. He said that he asked the practitioner to tell him what the ingredients are in the vaccinations.

The practitioner responded that there was no mercury in vaccinations and began reading the ingredients. After reading the first ingredient, Dr. Gyere stopped him. The first ingredient in the vaccination was Thimerosal. Thimerosal is an organic compound containing mercury.

The doctor elaborated on the effects of high testosterone and equated the level that Jordan had in his body with the levels of a 19 year old man. I couldn't believe it. The things that this man was telling us made sense, it all clicked.

He told us that he had a 9 year old patient who crawled under his chair and literally lifted the chair with him sitting in it, and threw it across the room. He said that the mother told him that she had been admitted to the hospital twice because of the injuries that her child caused.

After hearing Dr. Gyere's report and explanation we felt empowered. We felt like we were finally making moves towards understanding our son and helping him become successful. He ordered a battery of tests including full blood tests and urine sampling to determine the testosterone levels in Jordan's system.

It was a grueling process. It took over 3 weeks to receive the order to have Jordan's blood drawn.

Once we received it, we had to take Jordan to the LabCorp facility on four separate occasions so they could draw his blood. Jordan was a trooper though; he didn't cry or complain and allowed them to draw his blood with no problems. The company drew enough blood to fill a Red Cross blood bank, donation bag.

We waited on the edge of our seats for the response from the doctor. We were so anxious to find a pill, a serum or something to help Jordan that we were researching testosterone levels on our own.

Approximately two months later my husband received a call from the doctor informing him that he was no longer practicing medicine in Maryland.

He had been penalized or disbarred if you may, for questionable methods of practicing medicine. In my opinion, he was disbarred because his ideas and teachings had a negative impact on the pharmaceutical industry and since they have more money than anyone I know, they were able to make things happen.

This is of course only my educated opinion, but it really is something to think about.

They place ingredients in vaccines to ensure their longevity and their shelf life, not to ensure that the product is safe. It is up to us as parents to defend your children against harm, even if it is packaged and distributed in a harmless manner.

Okay, enough of my rant. I just become very passionate about these things. After hearing about the issue with Dr. Geyer we received Jordan's blood work results a few weeks later.

We poured over the results in search of something that would jump out and show us the source of the problem, to no avail. We did not locate anything out of the ordinary. Since we are not medical professionals, we forwarded that information to pediatrician in hopes that she could provide some insight.

I took a day of leave from work and we drove to the doctor's office. She evaluated Jordan and asked us questions about his behavior and mood changes. We showed her the results and asked for an explanation.

She glanced at the results for two minutes and handed the 20 page document back to us, simply stating, "I will wait for the doctor's review of his information".

My husband and I looked at her like she had lost her senses. We couldn't believe that she wouldn't interpret the results for us to understand. The blood work was filled with medical and genetic jargon that neither my husband nor I could decipher.

Once again we hit a road block. So, we found ourselves back at square one.

Read, Understand and Know Your Rights

As a Parent it is difficult to keep it all together. Many of us work full time; have more than one child and a family to tend to. On top of our other responsibilities, we have a special needs child. So what do you do when someone hands you papers and booklets detailing your rights as a parent of a special needs child? *Take your time and go through the entire booklet.*

It can be quite intimidating to join a meeting that includes educators, specialists and professionals.

Knowledge is power! You must remember that having knowledge about something gives you the strength and power to go on. Read the booklet, take notes and most importantly, ask questions.

How will you know if you never ask? Not all parents work in the education field and you are not expected to know everything about educating your child. However, it is your responsibility to understand the policies and regulations concerning your child's education.

We decided to have Jordan placed in a special center, within the school district where I worked. I arranged a meeting and a tour of the school through the principal. I was beyond excited, after visiting the facility. The center was exactly what Jordan needed.

They had a horticulture room where they taught the students how to care for plants and vegetation. They had a swimming pool and a large gymnasium. Overall, the most important thing about the facility was the principal. She was an angel. She took the time to explain the logistics of her school to me.

We met with the IEP team after I visited the school and told them about the school. I informed them that I wanted Jordan to attend the particular school and I also provided them with documentation and telephone numbers to facilitate the request.

The Special Education Supervisor swiftly informed me that we were unable to transfer Jordan from one public school system to another. She said that Jordan had to be transferred to a private school. She really felt that she was correct.

I informed her that she was not correct and informed her and the team that they could send packets of Jordan's information to public school systems and non-public systems to see who would accept him. I told her that as long as it was a Maryland school there was no reason why they couldn't transfer him.

She adjourned the meeting to call her supervisor to verify that I was correct.

When the Special Education Supervisor returned to the meeting she informed me that I was correct and they would be able to do just as I said.

This is why it is important to attend a meeting armed with information. Your information will provide you the confidence that you need to fight for your child.

I already knew that, but I smiled and left it alone. We were informed that the county employees wanted to visit the facility, before approving his transfer.

This information angered us. The previous school that they recommended, they had never laid eyes on, but now they have to visit the facility that I request. I let the anger go and continued to press on.

This is when you have a choice whether to be emotional and react immediately or to calm down and think about what's best for your child. It is easy to react quickly, and wise to think first. Being right isn't always the goal. The goal is the best education possible.

During the meeting it was decided that Jordan would remain on Home and Hospital teaching while we researched other schools and while they looked into Tanglewood.

After a week of non-communication from the school and the school system, I sent an email to the Special Education Supervisor and her supervisor requesting an update on the status of the visit to Tanglewood.

My husband and I wanted to visit the school, when they visited to ensure that we were all on the same page. ** *This is very important. You must ensure that there is a clear line of communication between you as the parent and the school. If not, they will try to bulldoze you and treat you as if you are the child. This is all a part of staying active in the process.*

We received a response two days after I requested information on the status, informing us that we would not be allowed to visit the school when they toured it due to the amount of people who would be visiting from the school system already.

I quickly informed her that we have the final say in our child's placement. I also informed her that we would be attending the visit and the individuals who they invited to tour the facility had no real clue regarding placement for our son, referencing their previous suggestion of placing him within an in-patient facility.

I was floored by her response. I couldn't believe that someone who was supposed to care about the students would hold up our sons' progress because of her own personal issues.

But instead of allowing my emotions and anger control me, I wrote an email. I also copied the Superintendent and the President of the Board of Education.

After I wrote my response to the Supervisor of Special Education, I then crafted a separate email for the Superintendent and the President of the Board of Education. As a result, I received a call from the Director of Human Resources.

She wanted to discuss the complaints and investigate my statement that Jordan was forced to remain in isolation throughout the school day. She did not want to discuss any of our other complaints, only the isolation issue.

While I was floored that they would not want to discuss our grievances in its entirety, I realized that something was better than nothing at this point. For Jordan's sake we needed results and a swift response.

When you are battling a school system, your first step is to identify the key personnel. Once you identify key personnel in the school system, you will have better luck at receiving a fair and just result. It would be beneficial for you to document a list of contacts, before a situation arises.

Then, when it is time to confront a member of the school system staff, you will know what avenues to take and who to copy on your communications.

I have also learned that written communication is best. It is best to email someone than call them. The primary reason for this is anyone can deny what they said, but it is more difficult to deny something in writing, originating from their inbox.

In my dealings with the school system, I learned that certain school system personnel will tell you anything on the phone, just to make you happy and get you out of their hair. In writing, you can make things stick.

An email is much more enforceable than he said she said conversations.

After repeated calls and messages to the Maryland Disability Law Center, we were finally able to obtain an advocate. She was phenomenal. We actually met her on the day of our scheduled IEP meeting a few weeks after we visited the prospective school for Jordan.

She informed us that based on Jordan's IEP and Behavior goals, they were trying to make Jordan conform to their rules and their environment instead of adjusting the environment to suit Jordan.

They were treating Jordan as if he was the problem in the classroom when actually they were supposed to be teaching and challenging him. It felt like such a relief to have someone agree that things were not progressing as they should.

It was wonderful. I took the time to inform the nine meeting participants that we were tired of them dragging their feet during this process.

I was angry and frustrated that Jordan had been out of school for 90 days and they were just beginning the process of having him accepted in a private school. I informed them that their time was not important and neither was mine, however Jordan's time was and they had wasted it.

90 days from the date that they removed Jordan from school, and the IEP team was discussing the process for moving him to a private school. It was totally unacceptable and I felt much better once I let them know, professionally of course.

Parents…there is no reason why you cannot voice your frustration and anger regarding the treatment of your children, as long as you it in a professional manner.

The school system offered to pay for Jordan to visit the KKI facility for the Intensive Outpatient Behavioral Program for three weeks. Initially, we declined their offer; thinking that we had health insurance that would cover the cost of the process. But our advocate clued us in on a few things. She informed us that with the health insurance, Jordan had a lifetime benefit allowance.

If we were to go through the insurance company for the Outpatient process, the money for the process would be deducted from his lifetime benefit. Surprised by this new information, we decided to allow the school system pay for the Outpatient procedure.

The school system informed us that while they would not pay for our stay in the hotel in Baltimore, they would pay for the mileage of traveling daily. We averaged the costs and decided to rent a compact car for the daily trip. We started Jordan in the outpatient center on December 19, 2011. We were nervous about the entire situation. We were ready for Jordan to return to school, with his friends.

Your Parental Rights

Every Special Education student has an Individualized Education Program (IEP) team assigned to them. *If your student does not, find out why they don't.* The IEP team includes the parents, teachers, specialists such as speech and OT/PT, Supervisor of Special Education and a School Psychologist.

Although, these individuals are experts in their fields, they do not know it all. You must be diligent and question the things that you do not understand. This is the point of the IEP team. So that everyone can meet and collectively agree on what is best for the student.

Did you know that as a parent of a special needs child you have the right to receive the *Maryland Procedural Safeguards Notice-Infants and Toddlers/Preschool Special Education and Special Education* booklet annually? You also have a right to receive the document in your native language. If you prefer the documents can be emailed to you.

As a part of Maryland State Special Education law you are entitled to receive prior written notice regarding planned actions of the public school. This includes early intervention services, changes to the IEP and discipline related changes.

Every child has a right to a Free and Appropriate Education (FAPE). This means that no matter the disability or issue your child deserves an education. If you feel as if your child is not receiving the FAPE that they are entitled to receive contact your IEP team.

It is best to meet with the team to ensure that your child receives the required services. Do not give up and Do not take "no" for an answer. If the public school refuses a service, question it. There is nothing wrong with not agreeing. It is how you disagree.

If you are professional and courteous in your disagreement you will get further.

Did you know that the public school agency must have written consent from you before they can conduct an evaluation on your child?

The school must inform you about the nature of the evaluation prior to conducting their assessment. The school must also obtain consent before they provide special education services.

Confidentiality of Education Records

Did you know that your child's education records are protected under FERPA? The Family Educational Rights and Privacy Act (FERPA) is a federal regulation that requires the school agency to maintain personally identifiable information in a confidential manner. You as a parent have the right to request your child's records, but the school agency must keep the information confidential.

As the parent, you have a right to review you student's educational records at any time. You also have the right to request that erroneous information be removed from the records. The public agency is allotted 45 days to respond to your request.

Discipline Procedures for Special Needs Children

As a parent of a special needs child you have certain rights that are afforded to you and your child with regards to discipline. The school may remove a student for no more than 10 days at a time for each violation of the Student Code of Conduct. *If a school agency removes your child from school for longer than ten days, they must provide educational services.*

Due Process Complaint vs. State Complaint

What happens when you realize that your child is not receiving a Free and Appropriate Education (FAPE)? Where do you turn? What do you do? First, you have to make the school system aware of the violations that you notice. If they make no attempt to correct the issue or they refuse to solve the issue your first reaction is to complain.

I'm not talking about the type of complaining that we usually do when something goes wrong. I am referring to proactively complaining.

How do you proactively complain?

First you document, document, document and document. I know it sounds redundant but documenting every problem, every attempt or failed attempt to solve the issue. This will only boost your case if it goes that far. If it doesn't, at least you are prepared.

Before you complain you must know how to complain and who to complain to. There is a State Complaint process which can be initiated by any person or organization. They can file a complaint alleging a violation or IDEA requirement. The State Complaint process is initiated by a written complaint.

The complaint can be typed as a letter or you can obtain a form from the Maryland State Department of Education (MSDE) website.

If you choose to type your own complaint it must include a statement that the agency violated a federal or State law, the facts that support the statement, the contact information and signature of the complainant and the name and address of the particular child. A State Complaint cannot be initiated after a one year of the violation.

Due process complaints must be initiated by the parent or public agency. The complaint can be filed in a manner similar to the State complaint process, but there are a few differences.

A parent can initiate a complaint up to two years from the date of the violation. You can obtain a form from the MSDE website or you may write a detailed letter.

Your letter must include your child's birth date, address, school location, public school system in violation and age. It also has to include the allegation, facts supporting the allegation and a proposed resolution to the problem.

No matter what you decide to do, I suggest that you have your letter reviewed by a trusted source. Sometimes an extra set of eyes can help you change the verbiage of your document for easier reading.

The public agency and IEP team must hold a meeting with the parents within 15 calendar days of receiving the complaint. The meeting must include a representative from MSDE.

Also, the public agency cannot include their attorney unless the parents bring an attorney. The purpose of the meeting is to discuss the facts and the complaint in an effort to resolve the dispute.

After the meeting, if the agency hasn't resolved the issue within 30 days, the parents or agency may request a due process hearing. Be advised that you can file multiple due process complaints. If another issue arises while you are working to resolve the initial complaint/problem, you have a right to file a due process complaint for that problem as well.

Seeking Legal Aid

So, what do you do when you have exhausted all available resources and you still are not satisfied with the outcome?

In short, you hire an attorney. There are a few things that you must do before you pick up the telephone to talk to someone. Search for attorneys in your area who specialize in Special Education.

These attorneys have a better idea of the education laws. They can also inform you if your case will ultimately cost or benefit you. While you search, make sure that you find an attorney who offers a free consultation. This will benefit you in the long run.

- ✓ Locate all pertinent information regarding your child (this is a great time to use your child's binder)

- ✓ Write down your criteria for an attorney. (Ex. How much are you willing to pay? Do you want a local attorney? Free consultation? Contingency?)

- ✓ Write down any questions that you would like to ask

  - o Ask about the attorney's experience with special education law, autism law or whatever you are looking for

- o   Ask about their retainer costs and any upfront costs

✓ Conduct an online search for attorney's practicing in your area.

- o   Narrow your search down based on the criteria that you previously set.

- o   Develop a list of at least three attorneys who fit the criteria, to contact.

✓ Contact the attorneys on your list

- o   Tell them everything, no holding back. The more they know the more they can assist you. Be honest. If their prices are too much for you, tell them. Often times an attorney will take your case on a contingency or pro-bono if they are confident that your case will win them something or publicity.

✓ Be prepared for disappointments. You may speak to ten different attorneys before you find the right one, but remember it is worth it. Stay encouraged.

Once Jordan was comfortably placed in a school, we had to decide if we should seek legal action against the school system. Their lack of knowledge concerning Autism jeopardized Jordan's education.

It was because of their lack of concern and knowledge that caused our 6 year old son to be at home for 9 months, with no education. We requested materials to tutor Jordan at home and they provided us with a bag of play money and a coloring book. We were furious.

He lost 9 months' worth of speech and language assistance and socialization. Nine months, which is well over 170 days of school were totally wasted.

The first attorney I spoke with was a fail. His suggestion was that if I sued the school system they could somehow stop providing payment to the new school. I disagreed an informed him that this would be considered retaliation under the law.

This is one of the reasons why it is best to contact several attorneys. Attorneys are not all created equal.

Some states will pay attorney fees if you win your case. Please keep in mind that you will not be awarded attorney fees for legal representation at an IEP team meeting, mediation conducted prior to the due process complaint or for resolution meetings.

Take a Deep Breath and Release!

Jordan started intensive outpatient therapy one week prior to the Christmas break. I had to work the first week of the outpatient process. I thought about Jordan and my husband everyday as they traveled the 150 miles to and from the facility. Then the following week, I joined them during the 150 mile trek.

The facility was great and so was the staff. We loved the fact that they offered valet parking so once we arrived we just hopped out of the car and walked inside. They worked well with Jordan. His first week went very well. The second week was not at all as we expected.

He grew tired of the outpatient treatment towards the end of the week and he truly began to rebel. By the end of the week, Jordan had lashed out at everyone who was working with him. We felt terrible. It was such a horrible thing to witness someone's arm being bit and scratched because Jordan wanted an escape. We were miserable and lost. We decided to end the treatment that Thursday and throw our hands in the air.

We didn't know what else to do. Jordan was definitely not going back to Baltimore. He would cry when we would merge onto 97 because he knew that he was heading into Baltimore.

We desperately needed help, but we felt like there was no one out there who could help us. We prayed for years on Jordan's condition, and our faith was waning.

Exhausted and defeated, we drove to my parents' house to pick up our oldest son. He was staying with my parents while we traveled to Baltimore.

We figured that it didn't make any sense forcing him to do the trek with us on his vacation. He would be better off sleeping in at his grandparents. At least someone would have an enjoyable Christmas break.

This was a low point in the lives of our family. Our parents and family were affected just as much as my children and husband by this situation. Everyone wanted what was best for Jordan and we all wanted to see him do well.

We were a miserable group of people for a few weeks, while Jordan continued with his treatment.

While this was a low point in our lives, it was also a pivotal point. I went through a period of reflection. I saw my husband as more than a caregiver. I saw him as our family's backbone. If he couldn't take Jordan to Baltimore while I worked and our eldest went to school, our lives would have fallen apart.

I was still able to work full time without using leave while Jordan attended his outpatient sessions, because my husband went above and beyond for our family. He chose to stay home with Jordan and work at night so our family wouldn't suffer.

I can admit that it was a hard four weeks, but it was well worth it. We learned how important we all were to each other. We learned that our involvement was key.

During the first few weeks that Jordan attended the therapy session, my husband and I would sit in the waiting room and read or play on the computer to pass the time. I used this time to work on my mystery book series.

During this time Jordan continued to get progressively worse. He acted out; he threw things and hit the staff at Kennedy.

——

When I returned to work and my husband had to make the trip solo, he became more involved in the sessions. At first, he would become upset when Jordan was having a bad day.

I understood his frustrations because we knew that Jordan could do better, we knew that Jordan was doing what he chose to do and in turn his behavior was affecting our attitudes.

I told my husband that I thought it was a waste of time to attend the sessions, but he thought different. I was being negative about the situation. My husband has a way of making me see the good in everything.

He had to help me see that there was joy in the present. When you focus on the bad things that's all you will see. He helped me understand that although things were not going great, I still had to keep the faith and look for the positive.

Since then, I have made an effort to change the way I speak and think. I stopped talking about how terrible things were, and started looking at the fact that our son was making small improvements.

True, he hadn't been in school since September and the school wasn't doing anything about it. True, we lost much more money than we could ever have imagined, but Jordan was improving and that was the major point.

With my husband's help, I changed. I changed the way I looked at the world. Maybe this was the whole point. Maybe this was God's way of informing me of what was really important and what was mute. We were aware that our life was as good or as bad as we wanted it to be. We couldn't control anything, so it was better to not try.

And the minute we let go and gave the situation over to God, fully, our lives changed.

My husband had an epiphany while driving home from one of Jordan's sessions. Since Jordan behaved so well for him, he would work with the team to assist with the Behavioral Therapy Sessions.

The moment he joined in on the sessions, Jordan took a turn for the best. He respected my husband more than anyone. So with my husband present, he didn't attempt to act out or behave the way in which he did prior.

Jordan began to pay attention to the Behavior Intervention Team. He began to allow them to work. Everything changed. Jordan was released from the program after three weeks. The program proved to be quite successful.

The team provided the school with recommendations on how to assist Jordan in the classroom. The school system refused to accept the recommendations and also refused to admit Jordan back into the program. They determined that he needed to be placed in a private school.

Although, it didn't seem like it at the time, this was the best decision they ever made for Jordan.

We visited many different schools during this time. We had to find a school that fit Jordan's needs. After months of searching we finally found the school for Jordan.

Back to School After 9 Months

Kennedy Krieger's Leap School was over two hours away from our house. We fought the decision to send him there for weeks. We couldn't imagine packing our six year old up and sending him two hours away from us, each day.

It didn't seem humane. We felt so alone. We felt like no one cared about our son. The school system would not budge. At this point, the Special Education Director and I were at odds and she was fighting every step we took.

We were at odds, in my opinion because I challenged their ill-conceived decision to remove our baby from school without a plan. From the moment they heard us voice our concerns, they were unhappy with us.

Jordan started school at Kennedy Krieger Institute's Leap School. We had to meet the bus at 5:30 a.m. My husband and I were so nervous. It was worse than the day I gave birth to him. We were on pins and needles the entire time. In fact, we fretted over it for days leading up to the big day.

We were relieved when we found that a dear friend of the family was the bus driver and the aide on the bus was the god-mother of my deceased sister. They both gave us hope. It felt like my sister was giving us a signal that it would all be alright.

Jordan had a great first day. In fact, all week he did very well. He had disruptions and aggressions. He hit a few of his peers, but it was alright. There was a difference in it all. The way the school handled it. I remember looking at the pregnant behavior specialist and feeling terrible when she described to us how Jordan acted. I couldn't believe that he was acting out in such a manner. He even took off his underwear and tried to flush them down the toilet.

But when I went to apologize to the lady she brushed it off. She told me that there were over sixty-two students at the school and each one of them has their moments. We felt much better. Since then, we have been gradually releasing our anxiety and concerns about the school thing.

There were a few issues, though. The bus ride is terrible. He is on the bus for over two and a half hours. He gets on the bus at 5:30 and doesn't get home until 5:40 in the evening. We are seriously considering moving closer to the school. We have to do something.

Every day we took a two and a half hour ride to Baltimore. We did this for three long weeks. When we tell others about our commute for Jordan, they shoot us a mortified look. How can you do that? They couldn't wrap their minds around the concept. For us, it was easy. Every day Jordan went to school we received a wonderful response from the teachers.

They were excited about his milestones. In fact, they once celebrated the fact that Jordan used the bathroom at school. It was a feat. The toilets flushed quite loudly and it terrified him. They celebrated the fact that he ate his snack at school. When his medication patch fell off during the day, they didn't call us. We couldn't believe it.

The three weeks that Jordan was at the school, they never called us. We were in awe. Each day for us in the beginning was torture. We worried when we put him on the bus, we worried about his day. When we arrived at the school, the teachers had smiles on their faces. Jordan wore a constant smile. That was all of the encouragement we needed.

Jordan's fast adjustment and willingness to go made us want to send him.

We remained in constant prayer that he would adjust. They told us at the school that their major goal was to get him to like school again.

Sadly, the situation involving his prior school made him literally hate school. He didn't trust anyone. The staff at Kennedy Krieger recognized that and made it their goal to change Jordan's mind about school.

It worked! The teachers and specialists at that school turned our baby around. From day one Jordan has loved that school. His behavior has improved and during his yearly review we were told that Jordan is their model student. Model Student! Can you imagine that?

His behavior charts are astounding. His behavior is no longer violent. He is no longer angry. He is a happier child. He loves going to school. In fact, if inclement weather causes school to be closed, we have a rough time consoling him.

He has friends at school. He can say his friends' names. It is truly amazing and we are so grateful.

We have faith in Jordan. We always knew that he would do spectacular things, but he is showing us now. His temperament has improved. He smiles more often. We can tell that he is happy to be back in a social environment again and seeing him happy, delights us.

Write About It

What is your passion? What comforts you in times of stress or turmoil?

It didn't matter what I was going through in life, I learned that writing about it always made it better. Personally, I carry three notebooks. One for my notes and one for inspirational quotes. I also write in a daily journal. I write to get out my feelings. We all know that being a parent of an autistic child is an emotionally trying experience. Many of us suffer in silence. We don't tell our friends or co-workers or loved ones how hard it is sometimes.

Writing is a fantastic option. There is no judgment in telling your feelings to a journal or diary. In fact, writing has become my therapy. I learned to write about everything. My bad days, good days, when there is nothing to write about, I still write.

There is nothing like having a rough day and reflecting on a diary entry from a good day. It helps you understand that it's only temporary. The feelings of frustration and anger are only temporary. I remember Jordan throwing my toiletries out of the window at our house once.

He couldn't be left alone. He would cover himself in lotion, Vaseline, hair pomade, anything. It was beyond frustrating. As he grew older we caught him baking his own French fries and nuggets. True, the oven was turned on 300 degrees and the food was only simmering, but he did it.

Detergent, salt, rice anything within reach was in danger of being tossed down the sink. Instead of blowing up, I wrote. I wrote about the times that Jordan emptied my plants of dirt. I wrote about the times that Jordan climbed inside of our pond and tried to swim with the frogs. I wrote about the times that Jordan used my $35 conditioner as a source of bubbles in the tub.

Jordan would climb trees with efficiency and run like an Olympian. To others he was exciting, majestic even. To me, he was just being himself. We no longer became surprised by the things Jordan did. He threw toys out of the window as we drove along the highway. Then he would have a tantrum because we refused to turn around and retrieve them.

The things that Jordan did deserved to be memorialized in writing. Like the Halloween party that we planned for the children. My sister had a crazy idea to throw a party for our children and their cousins. We had a house full of kids with music and sweet treats. I decided to make a creepy crawly cake. We decorated a vanilla icing cake with crushed Oreos and gummy worms. Once the kids finished playing games we returned to the kitchen to find a surprise.

Jordan was sitting at the table with the cupcakes. The topping was meticulously removed from each cupcake and placed on a separate plate. The cupcakes were perfectly white and showed no traces of Oreo cookie. As we stood in shock, Jordan carefully picked up a cupcake and placed it in his mouth.

The things that you write about don't have to be all pleasant. They don't have to make any sense. Honesty is the only requirement for writing effectively. When you are honest with yourself and your feelings, you forge a deeper connection with your soul and spirit. You know exactly what you want. When you know what you want and what you don't want, it is hard for others to sway you.

Talk About It, They will Listen!

Jordan did things that would infuriate me. He knew that we didn't want him playing outside alone, so he would sneak out of the house. We had to constantly keep the deadbolt locked and remain diligent. No matter how diligent we were, Jordan still found a way. One frigidly cold day, he came in the house completely covered in mud. He was soaking wet and dirty. I was so angry I didn't know what to do with him.

After bathing and chastising him, I went to my room and searched for my diary. I was at my wits end. That was when it happened. I finally broke down and contacted someone about my feelings. I called my sister and talked to her for an hour about my frustrations. She listened. She never interrupted me, she never questioned me, she listened. That made the difference for me.

Having someone there, listening to you is a priceless gift. Talking about your problems and your heart\aches help you heal. Writing is invaluable, but there is nothing like opening your mouth and expressing how you feel.

It is also difficult to talk to your partner. You feel as if they are going through the same thing, why remind them? Well, if you can't talk to the one in your home, then who can you talk to? Your spouse is the best sounding board out there.

Keeping the lines of communication open will only help you as you journey through the unexpected. This is true for raising any child. You must remember to talk it out. Believe it or not, there is someone out there willing to hear your story.

You must remember that no matter how hard it gets, you have to get it out. Keeping it in will only make you sick, believe me. Initially, I held my feelings in. I didn't tell anyone about Jordan or his situation. No one would understand, right? No, that is not right. There are people out there to support you.

I am an introvert, but even I found myself comfortable in group settings with other parents of Autistic children. I found that we had a common bond. We could discuss our remedies, trials and vent with each other. Support groups are a great option.

Take Time for You

Raising a child is an exciting and rewarding experience. Parenting is also a selfless job. It is hard to iron out time for your sanctity. You must remember to take time out for yourself, though.

How will you be any good to your child if you are burned out? Enjoying a life outside of your family is not a crime. In fact, I encourage it.

As a mother or father you have earned the right to leave your home behind for a few hours. I encourage vacations for couples away from their children. It doesn't have to be long, but you have to get away. It is imperative for married couples to vacation alone. This will help keep your relationship solid.

This is an opportunity for you to see your spouse as the person you married and not just the parent. Keeping your marriage in- tact and pleasant is a major goal in life. Your partner is your backbone.

No matter how hard we try, we always end up talking about the kids while on our hiatus. Over the years, we have turned it into a game. We tease each other whenever we mention the children.

Vacations away help you appreciate your children and your family. It is imperative for you to get away and have a release. I adopted a large repertoire of hobbies after Jordan's diagnosis. I found that my hobbies helped keep me grounded. I make it a goal to add a new hobby each year.

Since writing is my passion, I wrote four books. I also learned to sketch, no matter how elementary it looks, it was fun. I have taken swimming lessons, design websites and crochet in my free time. I am constantly questioned on how I find time to do these things. These things are essential to keeping me grounded. I need to write to remind me of the person I was before I had children.

Think about it. When it was just you, what made you happy? What hobbies did you have before having children? Once you find that out, you must act. Believe me, you will find a way to do what you love. Once you start doing what you love, you will be immensely rewarded.

This is a part of loving oneself. To love yourself you must find out what works for you. Then you must pursue it with a passion. After all, you are not on the earth to solely parent.

Forgiveness is a Gift

Once it was all said and done, I realized a few things. I realized that letting go and letting God take over was the greatest thing I have ever done. I also realized that forgiveness is a gift that I can give to myself. I no longer harbor negative feelings towards those who botched my son's education in public school.

As a Christian I cannot hold on to anything negative like that. If I don't forgive those who trespass against me, how can I expect God to forgive me?

Ephesians 4:31 says, "Let all bitterness be put away. Be kind to each other". Bitterness lies beneath the inability to forgive someone. Bitterness has an inherent effect on us. We are affected physically by bitterness. You can become so angry and bitter with someone that you internalize it. This will in turn manifest in illnesses such as high blood pressure, obesity and mental illness.

Bitterness damages our relationship with others. No one wants a sourpuss around, dragging them down. Remember that you cannot grow spiritually or mentally if you do not forgive.

So the next time someone hurts you, disappoints you or is downright evil to you, remember to let go. Look for the good in your pain. All things work together for the good. Through every trial and tribulation a lesson is learned.

Lose your anger and find your lesson.

The best part about it all, you will be more energetic and pleasant to be around.

Don' t Be Hard on Yourself

I know that when Jordan first received his diagnosis, I struggled through my periods of depression. I had plenty of outbursts and frustrations. I couldn't keep doctors' appointments straight. I had a tough time remembering Aiden's appointments as well as my own. I was a nervous wreck.

During this time, I was also working towards a Master's degree in Computer Science. I was in a bad spot when Jordan was initially diagnosed. A dear friend pulled me aside and had a stern talk with me.

She informed me that I needed to be easier on myself. She reminded me of the things that were filling my plate. She reminded me of how terrible I looked, but she also reminded me of something more important. She reminded me that I am stronger than I thought. I was ripping and running around so much, trying to make things comfortable for Jordan and Aiden.

I was wearing myself thin. I didn't take the time to think about what I was doing to myself.

I was placing too much on myself and not appreciating others. In better terms, I wasn't in a position to accept help. My family constantly reminded me that they would help with Jordan. They offered to keep him to allow my husband and me an opportunity for a break.

Instead of accepting their invitations, we made excuses. "No one will be able to handle Jordan". "He prefers to be in his home environment". The excuses continued. The crazy part, after all of the excuses were made we complained about being exhausted.

We realized that we were not using our resources effectively and it was damaging our relationship. We noticed that our lack of a break was causing us to become frustrated. Not only were we frustrated with ourselves and our situation, we were becoming frustrated with our lives.

That was when we decided to take the reins to our lives back. We decided to make the best out of our situation. We accepted the fact that we would always have to fight for Jordan. That was the reason why we were placed on this earth.

My parents could sense the feelings of frustration, depression and defeat in us. My father reminded us constantly that Jordan is destined for greatness. He reminded us of the story of his life.

As a child, my father was quite rambunctious. We often listened to his childhood stories and laughed with delight. Once Jordan began exhibiting his independence, my father felt the need to inform me of a few things.

He reminded me that he was once a strong willed, adventure loving child. Growing up as the oldest son of eight children, he was often chastised and punished for his behavior. He was very misunderstood.

You see, my father is the strongest, most intelligent hard working man that I have ever met. It was because of my father, that I was able to be who I am. He gave me direction and instilled drive in me. After listening to the stories that my father told, I felt quite hopeful.

That night, I prayed that God would have his way in my son's life. As far as I was concerned, if my son turned out to be anything like my father, he would be fine. I just needed reassurance that my son would have all that he needed to be a self-sufficient man.

I try to reflect on what my father says before reacting. This has really helped me improve my own quality of life. The level of patience that I have acquired for Jordan manifests itself in all areas of my life.

Instead of being angry about everything, I now embrace it. I don't get angry when I am cut off while driving; I just let off the gas and allow the person to go ahead of me. I don't get angry with my coworkers

Let's Talk About Video Games

I remember reading a story about a child collapsing after a weekend long marathon of video games, I panicked.

The wheels began churning in my mind. I knew that video games were not the greatest thing for children, but I felt that in moderation they would be fine. I didn't think about the affect they would have on Jordan or my nephew Kyle.

If you have followed my recent blog posts or if you are a parent of a child with traits like Jordan's, then you totally understand where I am coming from.

My husband and I had a discussion about Jordan's obsession and how to curb it. In the seven years that Jordan has been on this earth, he has taught us so much. Instead of reacting immediately, we try to take a step back and see things as Jordan would. This has been our greatest asset, leaning on each other.

This discussion started a dialogue about our own love for technology and video games. As I pondered over Jordan's love for all things Mario, I began to reflect on my own love for gaming.

My first introduction to Mario came at the age of 10. After months of begging, my parents relented and purchased me a Nintendo Entertainment System (NES) for Christmas. This was the first Nintendo game system ever.

I immediately took a liking to it. My children laugh at me when I tell them how excited I was to play games like Duck Hunt and Super Mario Brothers 1. Every day I rushed home from school to play my game system. I would play Super Mario Brothers from the time I got off the bus, until it was dinner time. After dinner, I was right back on the game.

I truly enjoyed it, but I didn't realize then that I was addicted. As a 30 year old female, I was a part of the first video game movement. There was no such thing as video game addiction in 1990.

Although, my family commented on how often I spent closed in my room playing with the game, no one stopped me. In the summer, I would try to play the game from sun-up to sun-down. My mother, an educator, put a stop to that quickly.

Before the NES I was a different child. I spent countless hours outside, playing and enjoying the fresh air. I remember times when I would leave my house in the morning and wouldn't return until I could hear my mother calling from the back deck for me to come and eat dinner. The minute the game controller was placed in my hands, that all changed.

I became obsessed with the game console. I played with the Nintendo well into high school. I was a senior in high school when my mother offered to toss the system in the trash for me. At that time, it wasn't that serious….I was dating by then.

I met a wonderful guy, who ended up being my husband and guess what? He also loved video games. In fact, I purchased the first Sony PlayStation for him as a gift. This renewed my love for video games like Mortal Kombat and Sonic the Hedgehog.

Jordan was only two when the Nintendo Wii came on the scene. Since my husband and I are both techies, we purchased the game system without hesitation. We introduced Aiden to the game system and he never looked back. The games allowed all of us to play at the same time. This became a part of our "family time" each night.

We didn't realize that Jordan was watching. Until the day we walked down the stairs to the basement and saw him sitting in the floor with a Wii controller in his hands. He was playing Super Mario Brothers Wii and he was enjoying himself. He clapped and laughed as Mario jumped on top of mushrooms and birds.

We noticed that he became quite skilled with the game system. This became a problem, because every time the Wii was turned on, Jordan came running. Aiden began to get frustrated with having to play the Wii in secret.

We purchased new Wii games as they were made available, but noticed that they were quickly becoming damaged. They had signs of scratches and scuffs on them.

We chastised Aiden about taking care of his things. He constantly defended himself, saying that it wasn't him. We learned the real culprit was his two year old brother, who we found holding the Super Mario Brothers game between his chubby fingers. To solve the problem, we purchased Jordan a Nintendo DS. This was the beginning of the end for us.

Over the years, Aiden migrated to the Sony PlayStation 3 games as his brother continued with his Mario obsession. To this day, Mario is the first word that falls out of his mouth in the morning and the last thing we hear at night. For years our nighttime rituals have included kissing Mario, "good-night".

I recall vividly the time we purchased Super Mario Party 8 for Christmas. This game allowed all four of us to play at the same time. I was Princess Peach, Aiden was Toadstool and my husband was Luigi, leaving Jordan who insisted on being Mario.

We soon realized that we couldn't play together. Jordan would breeze through the game, effortlessly. As he maneuvered through the game, earning coins and points, our characters died. You have to be able to see the other players to keep everyone alive.

We grew frustrated because no matter how many times we reminded him to slow down; he still breezed through the game. He would zoom through the game as if he was Mario; leaving all of our characters in the dust, to basically die. We gave up on playing the game together and let Jordan be.

This is when the battery issues began. Jordan realized that he could actually play all four characters by himself. So that's what he did. Well, if you are familiar with the Wii you know that the batteries in the controllers lose charge quickly. Since Jordan was supplying batteries to four controllers, we noticed a trend.

None of our remote controls had backs or batteries in them. Jordan figured out how to remove the back of the remotes to make the batteries easily accessible.

Our batteries in the remote control began to disappear. Have you ever picked up your remote and tried to change the channel, only to find it eerily light? We have. I remember vividly the first time Jordan spoke in a complete sentence. We were in Wal-Mart and I was pushing the cart while Jordan sat in the basket.

My husband and Aiden were helping with the groceries when we passed the sign, Jordan held out his hand. Then he spoke, "We need batteries!" he exclaimed. We couldn't believe it. He actually said an entire sentence. Then he leaned in the cart and grabbed a pack of AA batteries. The exact size for the Wii remote controllers. We were astonished.

Fast forward to today, batteries are now a hot commodity in our home. None of our remote controls have the back attached any longer. Jordan saw the covers as a deterrent.

He grew tired of asking us to remove the backs; only for us to refuse to do so.

We gave up on purchasing game systems. After seeing our fifth Nintendo DS purchase go flying across the room in the midst of a tantrum, we decided not to re-purchase. We re-purchased the Wii twice and countless Wii games.

I wondered if Jordan was in danger of some episode, since he loves playing his video games so much.

Initially, I conducted a search on video games with relations to seizures and other dangers. The information that I located varied in degrees of knowledge level and opinions of the author. Some experts and parents stated that video games were an inherent danger for children.

As an auditor, it is our nature to research even the tiniest detail in order to gain a full understanding. I researched the dangers of children and prolonged video game playing. I found that video games appeal to certain interests in many autistic children.

Video games are one sided, so you are not expected to be social. (Which are often times uncomfortable for autistic children) The flashing lights, quick movements and bright colors attract and maintain their attention. The game also offers a definitive start and finish. This helps the child feel as if they have completed something.

In my research I stumbled upon an interesting term, Photosensitivity. This is a condition that occurs in less than 3 percent of people with epilepsy. The flashing lights, quickly moving images and the prolonged play time can all contribute to an epileptic seizure.

While Jordan has not been diagnosed with epilepsy, it must be noted that nearly 25% of children on the Autism spectrum are susceptible to seizures. This really concerned me. Upon his diagnosis we immediately sought the expertise of a neurologist to ensure that he didn't have a propensity for seizures.

Most autistic children who have seizures usually begin to have them in their adolescence. This is believed to be contributed to the surge in hormones that occurs at the puberty stage.

While we were quite concerned, we also wanted Jordan to have a normal childhood; or at least as normal as possible. So in a way, we contributed to Jordan's video game/Super Mario Brothers obsession.

The name "Mario" is mentioned throughout the day and night, for any reason. When we would chastise him he would respond with one simple word, "Mario". This went on for months with us asking, "Why do you keep calling Mario's name?" He ignored our questions and quite frankly seemed amused by our perplexed faces.

One cold winter morning I chastised Jordan for running outside with no shoes on his feet. It was freezing out there, but Jordan could go outside naked in a snow storm and not feel a thing. As Jordan sat on the couch he angrily yelled, "Mario!"

I murmured under my breath, "Who cares about Mario?" just in time for my observant 13 year old to make an observation, "Mom, he thinks that Mario is going to save him" he said in a matter of fact way.

That was the turning point in our lives with Jordan. We learned that Jordan knew exactly what he was doing and what he wanted. After years of struggling and battling Jordan to make him do what we wanted we finally learned that it wasn't about us. It was about Jordan.

I stood there for a full minute with my mouth hanging open. How did I not think about this? He thought that Mario and Luigi would come save him from us like he saved Princess Peach from King Coopa.

At that moment I realized that the method of discipline was only causing distress for Jordan. From then on, we changed the way that we chastised Jordan. Instead of speaking loudly or sternly, we casually chastise.

We causally chastise by speaking in a normal tone and reminding Jordan of what we expect from him. He is highly perceptive so he can tell when we are not happy with something. Now he is at the point where he truly cares about what we think. He doesn't like to see us unhappy or frustrated by something.

The Optimistic Autistic Blog

We decided that our book wasn't enough. It was time to expand our knowledge and sense of sharing with the community. We decided to create a blog geared to helping others, while telling our story.

The Optimistic Autistic is a blog dedicated to the parents of special needs children. As a parent of an Autistic son, I explain tell our story. I suggest ways to cope with the Autism diagnosis, from a parent's perspective. We also interview parents of autistic and special needs children to help others on their journey.

This blog is about encouraging others and providing them with the tools needed to take charge of their children's education and lifestyle. The Optimistic Autistic blog is community based, focusing on fostering a supportive environment for everyone.

This blog is designed to help parents, educators and those who do not have a voice.

The Optimistic Autistic has proven to be more than just a blog for us. The blog has drawn input from across the nation. It is interesting to read others comments and hear their stories. After all this is why we are doing this; to share with others.

How will we be able to spread the word about Autism if we don't start with our own communities? Remember that we are all in this together.

Word on the Street – What' s Your Journey

This article was featured in our blog. We update the blog with current events and news. Each month we feature an interview with someone who is affected by autism. The goal is to share stories to not only inform others but to encourage them.

Welcome back to the Optimistic Autistic BlogSpot. Today we were blessed with the opportunity to meet with a parent who has not only inspired but encouraged us to keep fighting. Mr. Leonard has agreed to be interviewed by the Optimistic Autistic blog. Below is the transcript of our meeting.

OA: Hello, Mr. Leonard. Thank you for agreeing to be interviewed. How are you?

L: I'm doing well. Thank you for having me here.

OA: As a parent of an autistic child, I know that we all have unique journey's that brought us to this point. Tell us a little about your journey to this point.

L: Well, my oldest child was diagnosed with ADHD at the age of 4, so when Louis was born I was already on alert. I noticed that he reacted to certain things differently. He didn't like loud noises, he used to sit in the floor and place his toys in a straight line.

By the time he was three he hadn't spoken a single word. This was when I started to worry. We took him to a psychiatrist who came highly recommended. The psychiatrist informed us that Louis was on the Autism spectrum.

OA: Wow, what was your reaction to the news?

L: I didn't react initially. I didn't know what Autism was. I asked the doctor if there was a cure. He responded by shaking his head, "No". I couldn't believe it. I asked if there was something that we could do to help him. I received the same response. We went home from the appointment feeling hopeless.

OA: I can understand that. I know the feeling. When did it change?

L: I had an "Aha Moment" if you could call it that. I decided that. I realized that no one will care about my son and his success like us. His is our vested interest. If we don't stand up for him, then no one will. That is when we decided to get as much help for our son as possible. We started by contacting our health insurance company.

They gave us the names of speech and language pathologists that took our insurance. From there we set up 30 minute sessions for speech, twice per week. We drove there twice a week for speech. Louis did very well.

OA: That's great. What else did you do to help him?

L: Louis didn't have trouble with motor skills or being active. He is a very active child. We concentrated on his behavior and speech. Those two areas were totally affected by Autism. Once we began securing the help Louis needed we realized that Autism wasn't a debilitating illness. Instead, it had become the glue that held our family together.

           Our oldest son jumped in head first to help Louis. He played with him and talked to him as if he didn't have a special need. We placed the same expectations on Louis that we placed on our older child. We expected him to do chores and clean up behind himself. We made sure that Louis didn't feel different. I think that is one of the reasons why he is so independent today. We all worked to help Louis improve.

OA: So, how is Louis doing today?

L: He is doing well. He is enrolled at a great school, which is geared towards his special needs. He has friends and he knows how to play with them in an appropriate manner. We are proud of Louis. He has come a long way and we know that he has a long road ahead of him.

           But he has shown us so much. We underestimated Louis and he constantly surprises us with another accomplishment. Did I mention that he is talking in complete sentences? Who would have ever guessed that a doctor could be wrong? (Chuckles loudly)

OA: Thank you Leonard for sharing your story with us.

L: You're welcome. I hope that our family's story can inspire someone.

Interview with a Big Brother

We at the Optimistic Autistic find comfort in sharing our stories. We hope that you will find the same comfort. Each week we will interview someone different to find out how autism has affected their lives.

This week we caught up with Aiden, the ultimate big brother. Aiden is Jordan's thirteen year old brother.

OA: Aiden it is so good to see you. How have you been?

Aiden: I'm okay

OA: Well, the purpose of our interview is for you to share your feelings about having a brother like Jordan?

OA: Does he listen to what you tell him?

Aiden: Yes, he listens to me. He knows that he has to behave if he wants to play in my room.

OA: Is he a good baby brother to you?

Aiden: Sometimes.

OA: Sometimes he is good and sometimes he isn't?

Aiden: When he isn't doing things that are…like destructive like breaking my wrestling men or scratching my PlayStation games.

OA   What advice would you give to someone with a disabled sibling?

Aiden: My brother isn't disabled. He can walk, talk and think like any other person, he's just….Jordan. He knows what he wants and he does what he wants when he wants. (Shrugs shoulders)

OA: I know little brothers can be annoying, what types of things does Jordan do to annoy you? How do you cope when he damages your things or makes you angry?

Aiden: When he breaks something of mine I tell my mom and dad and they make him say "sorry". They replace whatever he breaks. He broke my Wii by putting pennies inside it. They bought me a new one. He broke my PSP game and a few weeks later I had a new one. I just try not to get frustrated with him.

He really is a cool brother and he does funny things. When I am annoyed with him I just close my bedroom door and he knows what that means.

OA: Well, thank you Aiden for talking with us today. You really are a great big brother!

Interviewing Aiden was quiet interesting. He is a typical teenager. His responses are short and to the point. I can appreciate that because you know that his responses will reflect his honest thoughts and feelings.

If your child has a sibling make sure that you solicit their thoughts on certain topics. You will garner much more support and better results from your children when they are shown that their opinions matter.

Tiger Mom or Purring Kitty

A few years ago, Amy Chua wrote a book labeled, "The Tiger Mom". In the book, she details and explains her strict approach to parenting, Chinese style. Tiger Mom style parenting involves expecting perfection because after all what else is there to expect. If a child does not perform to their optimal level it is assumed that they are not working hard enough.

The Tiger Mom spoke on expecting nothing but the best from her children. She talks about not accepting a hand-made birthday card from her child, because she felt that it wasn't her child's best.

Her children were forced to abide by strict and rigorous education schedules with little outside influence or contact.

Her children were not allowed to play video games or peruse through MySpace, YouTube, Facebook and Twitter. They were instead instructed to study, focus on their education and their talents.

As a parent raising a child in the USA, I understand that the Chinese definitely have an edge on education. We really need to increase our investments in the education sector, but that is a different story meant for a different book.

Chua's book became an overnight sensation. Not necessarily because parents supported her views, because of the amount of criticism that it received. Over the past few years we have heard many things about the "Tiger Mom".

This controversy has caused a massive debate that is still going on years after the book was published. Are we raising our children to be successful or are we raising them to be well-rounded? Which is more important?

As a parent who was raised by very attentive parents, I tend to lean towards the well-rounded part of my question. My parents were strict but not restrictive. They taught us how to act by their words and their actions. They drilled education into our heads and we listened. They expected A's and B's and nothing less.

I recall being grounded for two weeks for bringing home a "C" on my report card. True it was passing, but to my mother and father it was a sign of failure. As a child, I resented that, but I still worked hard to make sure that I never brought home another "C".

Fast forward to the new millennium, Aiden brings home a D in math and I immediately go into a tirade about how important education is. After weeks of punishments and the removal of the television from his room, we saw no progress.

We tried to encourage him to do better, but the things that we were taking away were only discouraging him. It was also hurting our family as a whole.

When Aiden couldn't watch television we all suffered. We like to watch movies together and play games together, but with Aiden on punishment we were unable to do those things. This is when it hit me. Punishing is not always the answer. My husband on the other hand has had a different approach.

He reminded me that everyone doesn't learn the same so why should our approach be the same as my parents? At that moment we decided to address Aiden's math and reading grades differently. Instead of punishing we created a rewards system.

Based on his daily grades, tests and quizzes, Aiden could earn computer time, television time and game time.

The incentive was as long as he tried his hardest he could do the things he enjoyed, on a limited basis. When he went above and beyond or brought home good grades, he would be rewarded with additional time. As parents we must take a step back and look at the bigger picture.

What works for one may not work for the other child.

What worked for you as a child may not work for your child. Our children are being raised in a completely different time than we were. They have more access to technology which is a great thing, but can also prove to be distracting.

We are raising our children to be self-driven, independent individuals. We tell them that they have choices and options. We give them options and then allow them to tell us what they want to do. I can't speak for all parents, but think about the choices and options that our children are faced with.

"What do you want for dinner tonight?" or "Where do you want to go today?" Do you ever recall being asked these questions as a child? If so, then you grew up in a much more democratic household than I.

Although we like the Tiger Mom approach it would not fit in with our home.

As parents we are faced with a set of options as well. You can take the advice of others and apply it where needed, but just remember that you are the person responsible for this child.

Their future rests in your hands.

Who will you entrust it too?

New School Year, New Plans, Infinite Possibilities

The onset of a new school year generally correlates to the onset of my stress and anxiety. Below are a few suggestions to help make your child's school year more successful and less stressful!

As you stood at the bus stop and waved good-bye to your student, you breathed a sigh of relief. The school year has begun, now you can relax, right? Wrong.

Now is the time for you to grab a cup of coffee and wipe the sleep out of your eyes.

The beginning of the school year is when the real work begins. When was the last time you looked at your student's 504 plan? Is it still applicable? What about your student's IEP? Are the goals still applicable?

Take this time to review these important documents. If you don't have any time to review them at home, take them to work or put them in your bag to review when you have the time.

While you are reviewing, keep in mind the changes that you have witnessed in your student. We as parents are the first to notice changes in growth and maturity.

If your student has been utilizing work books or a tutor over the summer, they may be more advanced than you think.

Maybe your student no longer requires a seat close to the teacher to hold their attention. Maybe you realized that your student requires additional assistance with their math work.

Was your student prescribed glasses over the summer? A new prescription?

If so, write this information down. This will be helpful for your student and for you in the IEP meeting.

The months of September and October can prove to be more important to your student than the last month of school. This is the time that you receive your first indication of your student's progress and abilities in school. This time is quite useful because you can see the 504 plan or IEP at work.

Schedule a meeting with your IEP team during the month of September to discuss your student's progress, your concerns and thoughts.

Remember to document your concerns and your thoughts in relation to your student's progress throughout the summer months and the school year. This will help you in ensuring that all of your concerns are addressed or at least expressed.

Remember that you are the first link in the communication chain. You are the glue that holds all of this together.

Not to put too much pressure on you! ☺ Smile

Use Social Media to Advocate for your Community

One day, Jordan hopped off the bus with a note in his backpack. His teacher noted that he didn't arrive to school until after 10:30 a.m. This was quite disturbing to my husband and me. We later learned that the school bus broke down on I-97.

For those unfamiliar with Maryland routes, I-97 is a busy route leading into Baltimore.

We were disheartened to learn that our seven year old autistic son was stuck on a school bus, on the side of the road for over two hours. Our initial reaction was hurt. We felt terrible that our seven year old son had to endure so much, just to receive an education.

My husband immediately contacted the transportation department to find out what happened. The director of transportation informed my husband that he had no idea that the bus had broken down. We inquired about regulations or procedures concerning school bus maintenance.

Only to be informed that no such procedure exists.

My husband was livid and so was I. After a few minutes of ranting and raving to each other about this massive problem, we decided to do something. *Anger without appropriate action is a worthless use of energy, in my opinion.* My husband decided to post a message on Facebook to just voice his frustration.

Within ten minutes of posting his message, we received an overwhelming response. I literally cried when my husband informed me that the community was supporting us. They wanted to protest and advocate for us.

There is nothing greater than the support of others for a common cause. People understood that autism is not just a personal issue it is a community issue. 1 in 88 children are diagnosed with Autism.

More children are diagnosed with autism than asthma at this time. Fair treatment of the special needs community is paramount, especially the little ones. Students like my son are not able to advocate for themselves. They are too young, but we can do something.

We can start a movement to ensure that our children are given the proper care and dedication. You must understand that Autism can affect anyone. It is not an illness that only affects certain races, ages, or sexes. It is much larger than that.

Result

As a result of our online campaign we were able to secure funding for transporting our son to and from school. Since our concerns included health related issues we secured documentation from our son's pediatrician that noted his weight loss and the possible effects of having him ride a bus for over two and a half hours each way without a bathroom break.

This information coupled with numerous articles helped us negotiate a better situation for our son. We were able to negotiate to have the school system reimburse us to meet the school bus. That option worked well, since the trip to meet Jordan's school bus was almost 130 miles round trip.

Jordan and I were accustomed to our routine, until one day things changed. On my scheduled pick up days, I would watch the clock eagerly anticipating Jordan's arrival. We would travel to any fast food restaurant he chose so that I could take him to the bathroom and grab him a quick snack.

After meeting the bus at our usual spot, I asked Jordan if he had to use the bathroom. To which he replied, "No". I knew that he had to go so I took him to the bathroom anyway.

Once we reached the inside of the gas station, he stood and gave me a look. "There" he said as he pointed to the "Men's" restroom. I told him that we would have to go to the girl's bathroom since I wasn't a boy.

Jordan refused to entertain the thought of going to the girls' bathroom with me. He stomped his foot and pointed to the bathroom door again. We struggled for a few minutes as I tried to reason with him. Then it hit me. Why am I reasoning with a seven year old about using the restroom?

I hesitantly knocked on the door of the men's bathroom and called out to see if anyone would respond. My body shuddered as I walked into the bathroom, calling out "is anyone in here?" I felt terrible. I tried to block all of the possible opportunities for embarrassment from my mind. I walked Jordan to the restroom with my eyes on the floor the entire time.

As we exited the bathroom, I walked into a gentleman heading in. he gave me a strange look and my eyes diverted to the floor. I didn't have the energy or the gall to explain anything to him. Instead I said a silent prayer, thanking God that he didn't enter the bathroom while we were in there.

Once we sat in the car I handed Jordan his snacks and took his binder out of his backpack. In his daily log I received the answer to my question.

The daily log indicated that Jordan recently completed a unit on family. There were pictures showing what a mommy looks like in comparison to a daddy. The pictures were identical to those that are on the door of the restrooms.

It finally clicked for me. Jordan was comparing the pictures and based on what he saw, he knew that he wasn't a girl. He decided in that moment that he didn't want to go to the girls bathroom. To date, he will not allow me to take him to the bathroom. I have officially handed over the duties of pick up to my husband.

It's truly amazing how much progress Jordan has made throughout the years. I saw growth not only in him, but also in us. We really learned about patience. Instead of reacting to what Jordan did we took the time to think about the real question. *Why did Jordan do something? What was his reason for behaving a certain way?* Once we took a moment to pause and think we realized that we had finally taken steps towards making progress with him.

Spiritual Interventions

As I mentioned prior, the church is a big part of our lives. When Jordan was born we stopped going to church regularly. We used to be so embarrassed when he would act out in church, to the point where we stopped going.

After years of searching, we realized that church was the right place for us to find peace and serenity. So we returned to our family's church. We were beyond nervous about the idea but we knew that something had to be done. This was a time where our faith was needed to get us through our situation.

It was quite difficult handling Jordan inside of a place that required silence and reverence. We decided to wait until he was at the age where he would know how to act.

Makes sense, right? Wrong!

We soon realized that we needed the spiritual foundation that we had growing up. My parents ensured that we attended church every single Sunday. As a child, I didn't fully understand it, but as an adult I know that I wouldn't be who I am without God in my life.

We tried to prepare Jordan for his first visit to church. We talked about it on Friday and Saturday. We let him pack a few of his favorite books and toys in his backpack. We packed bottled water and his fruit snacks to help him through service.

That Sunday, Jordan showed us how much he had grown. He sat through service with minimal effort. Of course he did some stemming and made a few noises. We ignore the noises and in turn he relaxed. The pastor asked if anyone felt blessed. Jordan stood and raised his hand. I can't tell you how happy I felt.

He stood and clapped along with the church members and seemed to really enjoy service. Our oldest son enjoyed it as well. My only regret was that I didn't take him to church when my grandfather was alive. He would have been beside himself to see the boy that he affectionately called, "hard rock" in church.

Since that first service, our family has been regular fixtures in church on Sundays. We have been careful about the distractions that we allow him to bring. As he becomes more accustomed to church and the routine, we remove items from his backpack.

Now, Jordan can sit through a church service without a book, a toy or a snack. This makes us very proud and it encourages Jordan. This shows his growth. Many moons ago, we wouldn't be able to sit in a mall food court without great effort.

Now, he is able to enjoy service without interruptions. Sure, he can be a hand full if service runs over, but we really see him trying to control himself. That in itself is terrific!

After church we make a big deal about Jordan's behavior. You would think that by now he would be tired of it. *Not Jordan.* He loves praises, so we pile it on thick.

We start it off by commenting on how well he behaved, then we give him a full round of applause for his great behavior. Although every day is not perfect, we want him to understand that there is good in everything and good in every day.

There is a lesson in this. The more Jordan attends church service the better he will be able to handle situations in which he has to sit still with very little stimulation or distraction. This makes a big difference.

We noticed that his behavior has drastically improved, in social settings. He can go to restaurants and sit comfortably while he waits for his food. In the past, we had to ensure that a cell phone, iPad or Nintendo DS was charged and at the ready. Now, things are different.

We are currently taking Jordan to swimming classes without any problems. He doesn't need to hold our hand when he is out. He can be redirected by verbal statements. It is amazing watching the transformation.

This has not only helped Jordan, it has encouraged us to include Jordan in more social settings. We attended a birthday party recently and it was amazing. For the first time in eight years, I was able to sit down with the other mothers and watch Jordan play.

I didn't have to follow him around or watch him like a hawk around the other children. I watched him play with the other children without a care in the world. In that very moment, I knew that we were on our way to something great.

We are also learning to relax more in social situations. This helps Jordan relax. He played with the other children without any issues. When we don't anticipate negative behavior, he doesn't display it.

We make sure to tell him how proud we are of his behavior. Praise is the best reward for him. We are supposed to learn something new, daily. Jordan helps us stay on our toes. The eight years that he has been on this earth he has taught me more than anyone could.

The most important thing he taught me was how to be unapologetically me. Jordan has given me the courage to step outside of my comfort zone.

It was because of him that this book exists. It is because of the turbulent time in our lives, that I was able to write four books.

My quest for an escape, lead me to fulfill my dream.

Thank you, Jordan!

Reflections

Jordan is heading into his second year in private school and he is excelling. We are not at the finish line, yet but we definitely are not where we started.

Having Jordan in our lives has enriched it more than anything. He has helped us see every day as a new experience. Jordan keeps our lives quite interesting.

There is no stronger love, than the love that we have for our children.

Although, it may seem hard and the task may seem daunting, we must hang in there. We must fight the good fight for our families.

The times when Jordan was out of school were the most miserable times of our lives, but something fantastic came out of it. It renewed our faith. We literally saw how God moved, the minute we let it go.

He showed us that we don't have to worry about tomorrow. We don't have to worry about today. We just have to trust that it will be okay.

Our family is better, stronger and happier because we went through the thick of it together. We stand taller knowing that Jordan is happy and successful.

We are proud that Aiden has grown into a loving, caring, bright young man. Our life is not perfect, but we made it through the bad times and we're still smiling. That says a lot.

We hope that you enjoyed reading our story. It is our prayer that you are more encouraged now than you were before you opened this book.

Please remember God's promises for your life. When you are discouraged remember that he will not give up on you. He will finish the work that he has begun.

Just when we thought we couldn't handle it anymore, Jordan showed us that we were stronger than we thought. He showed us what unconditional love really is. He is enjoying himself and we can literally see a change in him.

Amazing things happen when you learn that you cannot control anything and you let God take over. Once you realize that you are not in control, you begin to see just how beautiful life really can be. I encourage you to push on.

When things look like they won't get better. When the teacher is calling daily or sending home notes that your child is misbehaving, hang in there. It will get better.

The purpose of this book is to give you hope. To remind you that better days are on the horizon.

When you think no one hears you, *we hear you*. When you think that no one will understand; *know that we understand*. Like you, we have experienced horrible days, but we have also experienced joyous days.

When you sit back and look at your life, you have many things to be grateful for. Be grateful for your situation and know that there is a reason that you were given this special child. Special children are only given to special parents.

Be Blessed!

Sage

The Optimistic Autistic BlogSpot

: http://www.optimisticautistic.com/

Check out our blog: **http://www.optimisticautistic.com/** for more information, stories, interviews, discussions!

Share your thoughts and opinions with us.

Together we can create a great future for the special needs community.

References

Ball LK, Ball R, Pratt RD. An assessment of thimerosal use in childhood vaccines. PEDIATRICS 2001;1147-1154.

Parental Rights – Maryland Procedural Safeguards Notice – Infants and Toddlers/Preschool Special Education and Special Education www.marylandpublicschools.org Rev. January 2010, Effective February 1, 2010

http://theoptimisticautistic.blogspot.com/

www.ingramcontent.com/pod-product-compliance
Lightning Source LLC
Chambersburg PA
CBHW070527030426
42337CB00016B/2137